# FORTUNATE MEMBER OF A CARIBBEAN DIASPORA

## PHILIP TIMOTHY ARNELL

Copyright © Philip T. Arnell

The moral right of the author has been asserted.

All rights reserved.

No part of this publication may be reproduced, stored in a retrieval system, or transmitted, in any form or by any means, electronic or mechanical, by photocopying, recording or otherwise, without written permission of the copyright owner.

# Prologue

Hello All,

I present to you a book of my families' history based on available information, both recorded and personal account. It has taken centuries to create; however, 34 years of compiled information I present to you. In this book you will learn about who our ancestors were, where they came from, and where it has led us all to today. Our family has spanned the globe through our bloodlines, our migrations, and Off Springs. Embrace your lineage, learn as much as you can about all of your cultures, and pass all of this information on to our generations now and for those to come. Our ancestors, including our parents have lived through the toughest of times, progressed, and managed to keep our family together. The family adage of those before us, has been ***"We made it through the worst of times, and we all made it through"***. This log is dedicated to the memory of all those who were here before us, walked among us, and who eventually had to leave us both young and old.

We can continue to excel in the future if we all strive to know all of our past. It is said that to know yourself and to be complete, learn, accept, embrace and treasure where you came from. Never let your culture leave you.

Learn, Appreciate, and Enjoy!

## Philip Timothy Arnell

# The Carty/Hodge/Webster/Hazel/Lake Families

# ANGUILLA, BWI

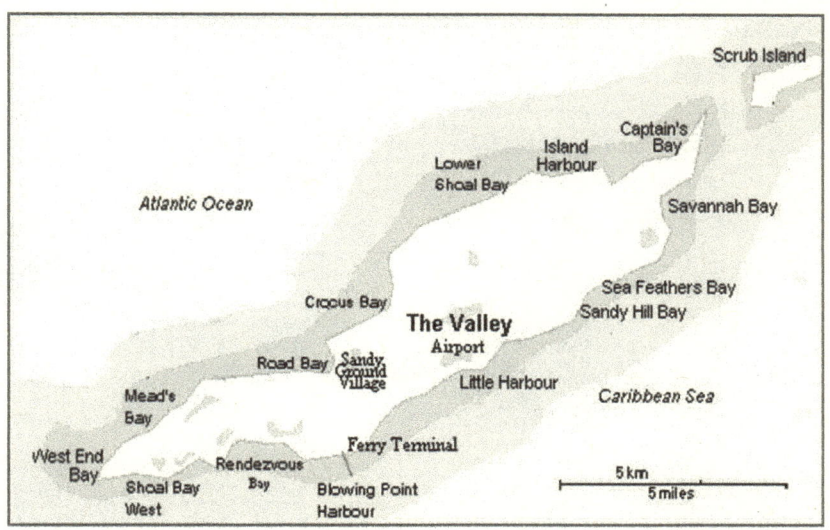

Anguilla

The United Kingdom

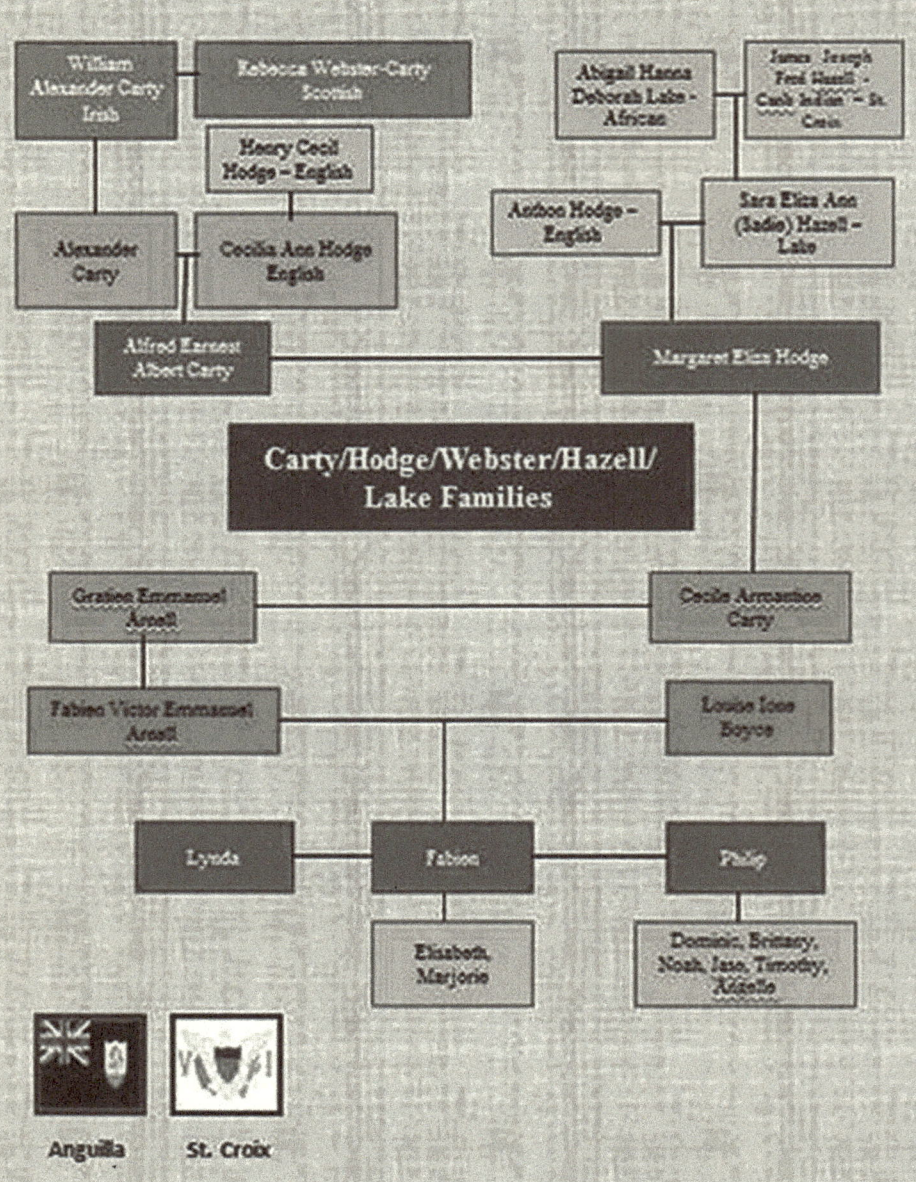

# THE CARTY/HODGE/WEBSTER/HAZELL/LAKE FAMILIES OF ANGUILLA, BWI

**Margaret Eliza Hodge (Grandsall):** Born in Anguilla approx. 1866. Her mother **Sarah Eliza Ann Hazell - Lake** was born in Anguilla, 1840. Her father was **Anthon Hodge (B- 1839)** of Island Harbor who was of English descent. Sarah's parents were **Hanna Deborah Lake (B – 1810)** of African Descent. Her father was **James Joseph Fred Hazell (B- 1824)**, a Carib Indian originally from **St. Croix – Danish West Indies**. Sarah's Indian name was known as "**Mooma**". For the first few years of Margaret's life she resided in St. Croix. In 1870 Sarah Hazel-Lake returned to Anguilla with her sister Johanna "Donie", and her daughters Johanna, Margaret Eliza (**Grandsall** – who was 4 years old at the time), and Ann Elizabeth.

How they ended up living in St. Croix was due to the fact that many Anguillan's went to different islands for work related reasons. When the work was finished, many returned. Her mother Sarah remained in Anguilla until her passing in 1893 at the age of 53 years old from "Brights Disease". In today's world it is known as a form of kidney disease known as "Chronic Nephritis".

Grandsall was also related to the famous General Hodge which led the famous brigade against and won the war from the French as they tried to claim the island through Rendezvous Bay Beach (Located on the West End of the island). She was one of 7 children (one of 3 by her mother, there were four others by her father, falling in the middle).

Grandsall married **Alfred Earnest Albert Carty**, they married approximately between the ages of 17 and 19 years old on September 11, 1884. Together they raised 12 children until Alfred's untimely death in 1907.

As a schoolgirl she was given the nickname of "Crazy Sall" and "Sally" due to her love for playing practical jokes. The name stayed with her throughout her life in which to this day she is still referred to respectively as " Grandsall". The area where the family resided was known as Chalvilles Hill in the Welches Region. But many refer to it respectively as "Grand Sall Hill". She died in 1952 at the approximate age of 86.

The Carty Family of this era was one of the elite families of Anguilla. One of the families of "Webster Yard" of the East End. They had two houses, one at the top of the hill, and one at the bottom which were surrounded by a considerable portion of land (about 140 acres). Up until about 1990 part of the original structure of one house was still standing. Until approximately the mid 2000's the original structure of the cistern that was built in 1930 by Gratien Arnell (the husband of Cecile Armantine Carty, the Carty's 11th child) was dismantled. The cistern was in full working order until its final day.

**Alfred (Feddy) Ernest Albert Carty:** Born in Anguilla in 1865, his family originally came from Ireland and Scotland. He was born and resided in the Lowlands area of Anguilla East End. The family's name was originally **McCarty** originally from Ireland, in Anguilla it was changed to Carty. His grandmother Rebecca was originally from Scotland who arrived in Island Harbor approximately around 1790, her surname was **Webster**. He was a planter by profession. He died an untimely death in 1907 due to a urinary tract infection at the approximate age of 42 in the family house on Chalvilles Hill, located in Welches.

## Alfred's Grandparents:
**William Alexander Carty** – B – 1778

(William's Siblings – Eugene b – 1787, Franky, Theophilus, and Phillis)

**Rebecca Webster Carty** – Arrived in Island Harbor approximately in 1790 from Scotland.

## Their Children:
**Alexander Carty** – 1800 – 1878 (**Alfred's Father**)

John – b – 1796    Ludwig Reginald - b – 1801

Lovelace – b 1809    Amanda - b – unknown

## Alfred's Parents:
**Alexander Carty** – 1800 – 1878

**Cecilia Ann Hodge** – 1842 – 1937

(Cecilia's father was **Henry Cecil Hodge**)

Alexander and Cecile moved to Sint Maarten in 1878, where they remained for the rest of their lives. Both were buried in the Methodist Cemetery on Front Street.

## Alfred and Margaret's Children: 12

**Clementina Gumbs** - April 28, 1882 - 17 children
**Sarah Ann Melvina** - May 17, 1885 - 8 children.
**Victoria Albertha** - December 29, 1886 - 10 children
**Alfred Lewis** - May 31, 1888 - 1 child.
**Jane Clothilda** - November 10, 1889 - 5 children.
**Ernest Albert** - March 11, 1892 - 3 children
**Laura Joseta** - August 1, 1893 – 17 children
**Patronella Dalton** - June 5, 1894 - No children.
**Eldridge Campbell** - December 3, 1896 - 1 child.
**Wilfred Manchester** - March 11, 1898 - 3 children
**Cecile Armantine** - January 16, 1900 - 6 children.
**Aise Viotee** - March 29, 1902 - 3 children

Margaret Eliza Hodge-Carty (Grandsall)

**The area formerly known as Chalvilles Hill, Anguilla, named after Grandsall.**

Final resting place of Margaret Eliza Hodge Carty (Grandsall). Sandy Hill Cemetery, East End, Anguilla.

The Carty/Hodge family church
St. Augustine's Church
Sandy Hill, Anguilla.

# The Children of
# Alfred Ernest Albert Carty and
# Margaret Eliza Hodge - Carty

Victoria Carty – Flemming

Alfred Lewis Carty

Laura Joseta Carty – Saunders

Othniel Saunders (Lauras's Husband),
Founder of the East End School

Jane Clothilda Carty - Hunt

**Wilfred Manchester Carty**

**Patronella Dalton Carty**

**Eldridge Campbell Carty**

**Ernest Albert Carty**

Cecile Armantine Carty – Arnell

**Cecile Armantine Carty Arnell:** Originally from Anguilla, BWI. Up until 1996, she was the sole survivor of this immediate Carty family. She was the 11th of the twelve children. She is remembered as one of the great educators of Anguilla where she was a school teacher at the "East End School" until 1930. Many of the present day older generations of Anguillians were her students. To this day she is still referred to as "Teacher Armantine". ☺). In 1930 she married Gratien Emmanuel Arnell of Saint Martin, FWI, and together they had 6 children, Maria, Rodrique (Rico), Fabien, Nicholas, Armelle, and Cassie. She is mostly responsible for the historic facts provided for this portion of our history log (thanks Grams). She passed away on July 8, 1996 at age 96, in Queens, New York. Her last surviving sibling was her sister Jane Clothilda Carty Hunt, who resided in French Cul De Sac, Saint Martin until her death in 1987, aged 96. The Carty/Webster/Hodge/Hazell/Lake families live on throughout the world generation after generation due to the vast number of offspring.

**Family Names:**

| | |
|---|---|
| **Carty** | Rodgers |
| **Hodge** | Smith |
| **Webster** | Ruan |
| **Hazell** | Connor |
| **Lake** | Brooks |
| Gumbs | Flemming |
| Harrigan | Carter |
| Hunt | |
| Vanterpool | |

**\*Bold print signifies direct bloodline**

# Birth certificate of
# Cecile Armantine Carty - Arnell

| No. | When Born | Name (if any) | Sex | Name and Surname of Father. | Name and Maiden Surname of Mother. | Rank or Profession of Father. | Signature, description and residence of Informant. | When Registered. | Signature of Registrar. | Baptismal Name if added after Registration of Birth. |
|---|---|---|---|---|---|---|---|---|---|---|
| 2383 | Jan 16 1900 | Cecile Amentine | Female | Alfred E. Carty | Margaret E. nee Hodge | | Alfred E. Carty x Planter Spring Down | Feb. 10 1900 | A.H. Ebenter | |

BIRTH in the Parish of _____ in the Island of Anguilla in the Colony of St. Christopher Nevis Anguill.

I Certify that the above written is a true Copy of the entry in the Register Book of Births in the Parish of _____, in the Island of Anguilla

BOOK No. 2 Extracted this 17th day of February, 1966

The East End School
where Cecile Armantine Carty – Arnell
taught many early Anguillian's until 1930

# Aise Viotee Carty

## Patronella and Aise – later years

# Carty/Hodge/Webster/Hazell/Lake Family/Origins

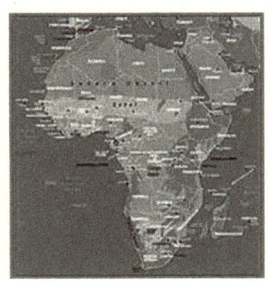

Africa

Ireland

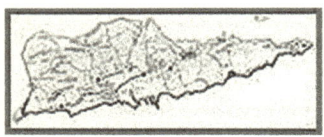

St. Croix

United Kingdom

Scotland

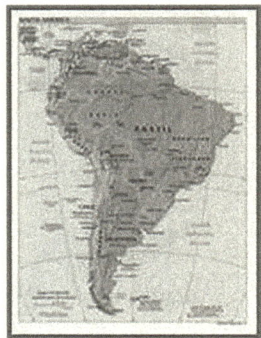

South America

# Saint Martin F. A./Sint Maarten N.A

## Saint Martin F.A. / Sint Maarten N.A.

Saint Martin

France

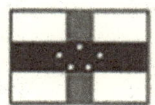
Sint Maarten

Holland

# The Richardson/Hughes/Baly/Barrington/Rovlet/Brooks/Arnell/Guy/Howell/Arrindell/Bebroudt/Pantophlet/Calvert/Ruan/Gumbs/Laurence Families

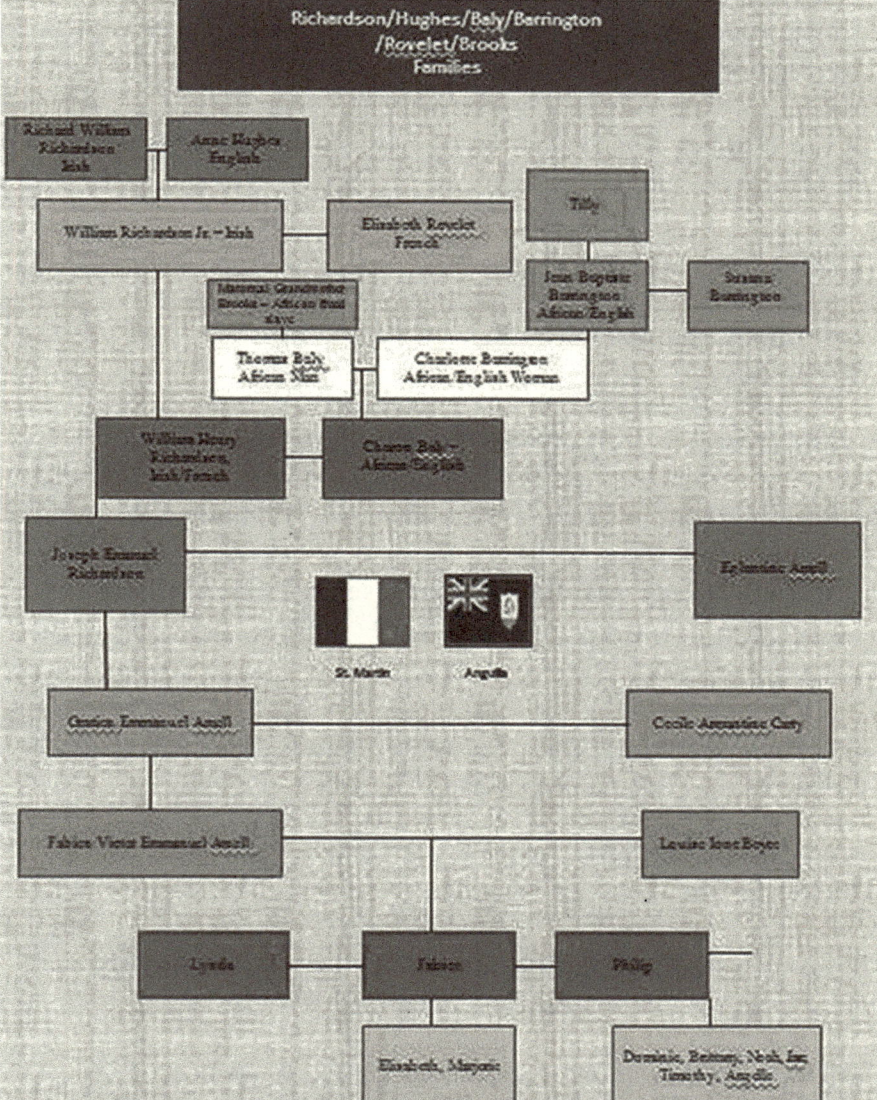

# THE RICHARDSON/HUGHES/BALY/BARRINGTON /ROVELET/BROOKS FAMILIES OF ST. MARTIN, FWI/ANGUILLA

**Richard William Richardson–** birth unknown– Irish - born in Anguilla, died in 1797 in Nevis.

**Anne Hughes** – birth unknown– English - born in Anguilla, died in 1814 in Anguilla.

**Their son:**

**William Richardson Jr.** – Born 1792 in Anguilla/ Died April 3$^{rd}$ 1893

**Anne Deborah Hodge (William's first wife)–** Born 1815

**Children:** Horatio, Mallery, Ann Elizabeth, William, Jack.

**Elizabeth Betsey Rovelet (William's second wife/William's mother)–** Born 1815 / Died March 9$^{th}$, 1878– Rambaud, French descent

**Children: William Henry,** Adolphus, Sophie, Louisa, Jeanette, Felix, Robert Albert, Anne Marie, Clemence.

**Ruth Bryan (William's third wife) – Born 1820**
**Children:** Julie Rebecca, Susanna

**Frederika Richardson (William's fourth wife) – Born 1818**
**Children:** Jean Baptiste, Leon Alexandre

**Victorine Poumon (William's fifth wife) – Born 1830**
**Children:** Virginie, Eugene Virgile, Ernestine, Madelonette, Marie, Claudine.

### William Jr. and Elizabeth Rovelet's son:

**William Henry Richardson:** Born August 14$^{th}$, 1838 / Died November 30$^{th}$, 1902.

A tailor/mattress maker by profession. Resided in Rambaud, French St. Martin.

### William Henry's Wife:

**Carron Baly: 1845- 1915** - She was born in Rambaud, French Saint Martin. Her mother was **Charlotte Barrington** of St. Martin, FWI. Charlotte's parents were **Jean Baptiste Barrington** and his wife **Susanna**. Jean Baptiste's mother's name was **Tilly**. Carron's father name was **Thomas Baly – Birth appox. 1819**. His maternal grandmother was a freed slave whose surname was **"Brooks"**. He was a highly respected man of his village and was looked upon as a captain of the town. Carron's death was due to a heart attack while doing a traditional African Panum dance at a family gathering in 1915. She was affectionately known as **"Dede"**.

### Children:

Alfred (B-1868), Claudine Isolene (aka Mamezelle) (1872 – 1968), Joseph Emanuel Richardson (1874 – 1949), Elisa Ines (B- 1881), Willie, Philippe Auril Anatole,
Zelia, Alice, Boonie, Joseph Cagan

There were other outside children through William, one named Nathaniel. Other than him, there is no available information on them.

**Joseph Emanuel Richardson: October 16, 1874 – May 8, 1949.** Born in Columbier, French Saint Martin in 1874. Raised in Rambaud. He was a politician which held the title of the Governor's secretary to the Marie, and of the office of the port of St. Martin, FWI for many terms. He lived in the Concordia Section of Marigot with his wife and 8 children. It is said that he had fathered 59 additional children outside of his marriage in which he took full responsibility for all and put them all through school. He had 2 children with Eglantine Arnell of French Cul De Sac, Gratien (Mannin) 1905 - 1981, and Marie 1912 - 1991. He resided in Marigot until his death in 1949 at the age of 75 of a prostate disorder.

It has been said that somewhere within the Richardson family there is Asian lineage. The physical characteristics are present, and many have attested. Research is still being conducted. Facts are elusive, but efforts will be continued. Of the many children of Joe Richardson, there are still some survivors. The family is tremendously large, and has spread throughout the world.

**Family Names:**

**Richardson**
**Hughes**
**Baly**
**Barrington**
**Rovelet**
**Brooks**
Lewest
Flanders
January
Barrot
Duruo

**\*Bold print means direct bloodline**

# Death Certificate of William Henry Richardson

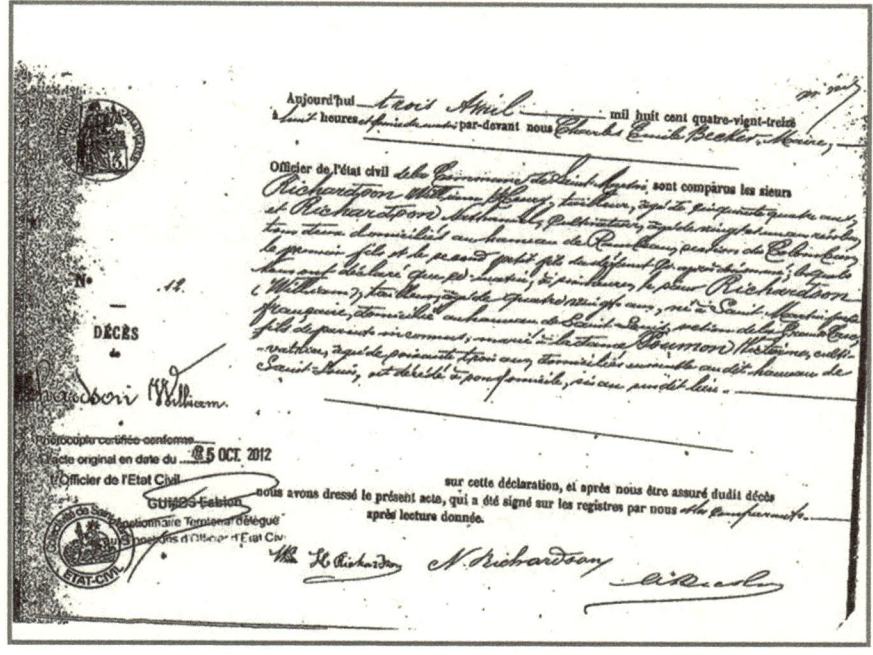

*Joseph Emmanuel Richardson*

Joseph Emanuel Richardson (Bon Papa)

Later Years

Because of his long term of civil service, Joseph Emanuel Richardson was decorated and received the Cross of the Legion of Honor, along with the decoration of Merit for Agriculture.

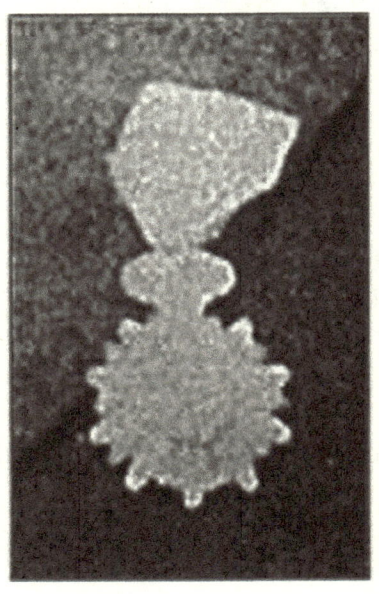

Present Day Version

Claudine Isolene Richardson
aka "Dit Mamezelle"
Older sister of Joe Richardson

# Home of Joseph E. Richardson, Concordia Springs Marigot, St. Martin, FWI

The street adjacent to his home,
named in his honor

# Final Resting Place of Joseph Emanuel Richardson Marigot, St. Martin F.A.

Ici – Repose
Joseph Emanuel Richardson
Secretaire Municipal, Chevalier De L'Ordre Colonial
Decede A St. Martin,
19 Mai 49A Inge 75 Ans

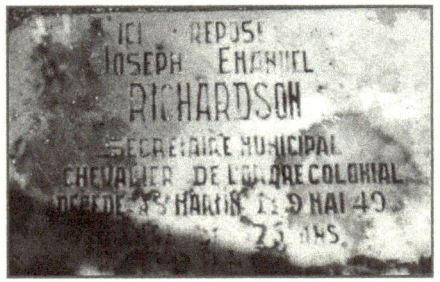

Translation: Here lies Joseph Emanuel Richardson
Municipal Secretary, Knight of the Colonial Order.
Died in St. Martin, May 19, 1949, 75 years old.

# Marriage Certificate
## of Joe Richardson and Marie Dessout

# Death certificate of Joseph Emanuel Richardson
## Place of Death – Sint Maarten, Netherland Antilles

Heden *negen Mei* negentienhonderd *negen* en veertig verscheen voor mij, hulpambtenaar van de burgerlijke stand op *Sint Maarten, Larmonie, John Charles*, oud *negen en veertig* jaren, *Officier der Veldwacht*, wonende alhier, die verklaarde, daarvan uit eigen wetenschap kennis dragende, dat op *negen Mei* dezes jaars, des *voor* middags te *half tien* uur, alhier is overleden *Richardson, Joseph Emmanuel, in de ouderdom van vier en zeventig jaren, zonder beroep, geboren en wonende op Sint Martin Frans Gedeelte, echtgenoot van Gumbs, Marie Elizabeth Pauline, zonder beroep, zoon van Richardson, William Henri en van Baly, Sharon, beiden overleden.*

Waarvan akte, welke is voorgelezen.

## Marigot Catholic Church, St. Martin, FWI

The church where Joseph Richardson played the violin for the church choir and the congregation.

The Richardson Family Church
Ebenezer Methodist Church
Marigot, St. Martin, FWI

# Children of
# Joseph Emanuel Richardson

# Paul Joseph Amedee Richardson

From the Memoirs
of Paul Joseph Amedee Richardson.

# Mini – Stories Of The Past
# By Paul Amedee Richardson

## My Father Joe Richardson

My Father was Joseph Emanuel Richardson. Who was the fourth son of his parents was born at Rambaud on October 16th of the year 1874.

After his school years he went to work at the age of 14, in the farm of his father. When he was 18 years old, he was chosen by Mr. Charley Baker, the Maire of St. Martin, to work as a clerk in the maire. Four years later he was promoted after the death of Mr. Dewer, the municipal secretary. He became his successor. As the first colored man in his position, he served the community in this capacity for 50 years, in combination with other jobs. So from 1908 until 1946 also harbor-master, in which capacity he was honored for having saved the island from an epidemic of smallpox by his severe control of the bill of health from the neighboring islands. Also he served for many years as an interpreter in the Court of Justice and during the First World War in 1914, he got the function of military reporter.

As a municipal secretary, he was called, "the father of the people", due to the fact that he was always at their disposal for any advice, especially in judicial cases. Due to his long term of service he was decorated and received the Cross of the League of Honor. He also received a decoration of Merit for agriculture, for though he had become an office-man he remained a cultivator which he was by birth. Through his good knowledge of farming, he was able to help advance the farming in St. Martin. He himself was growing onions, carrots, beets, cabbage, while he was also raising cattle, horses and mules, and was famous on the island for his fresh butter.

# Mini – Stories Of The Past
## By Paul Amedee Richardson

## The Grandmother Who Died While Dancing

My grandmother from father's side was Carron Richardson-Baly. She was born in 1845 at Rambaud as the daughter of Thomas Baly. Also this great-grandfather I can remember very well. He was a smart old man. In Rambaud, he was considered as ruler of the village. He was a local preacher of the Methodist Church, but after some insult, he was no longer on speaking terms with the Minister, so he used to come to Marigot every Sunday and go to the Catholic church with us.

He was a good farmer and producing meat was one of his favorite jobs. But above all, he was an old time musician who played with much bravura the violin, which he called the fiddle. his wife was Charlotte Barrington, born on St. Martin. They had 2 children, a daughter Carron (my grandmother) and a son Camille, who followed in his father's footsteps in agriculture and in music as well. My great-grandmother Charlotte was very good looking and a devoted wife. I can remember that when she had to serve her husband his meals, it was done with so much of Grace. She would put every dish before him containing different parts of the meal and let him Choose what he liked the best.

When we, their great grand-children (5 of us, myself included) were sitting at table too, he would see to it that she served all of us first and then himself. He would say the blessing before the meal, and his wife after the meal.

Their daughter was Carron, my grandmother. She died in 1915, 70 years of age, following a heart attack while dancing with a young girl, showing her how they used to dance when she was a young girl. It was the evening of Easter Monday.

The day before, after the Easter Mass, she had come to our house to see her granddaughter (My sister Josephe) play the piano that my parents had bought shortly before. She then said that she was glad to see one of her descendants doing what normally only the white people used to do.

# Mini – Stories Of The Past
## By Paul Amedee Richardson

# My Grandmothers' Funeral

After my grandmother had suddenly died in 1915 while she was dancing, a cousin of my father, Charles Richardson, who was the Brigadier of the Police, came to Marigot and entered our yard. He came to the gallery where my father met him at the door. My father said, "I know what is the news you are going to tell me, Dede is dead." "Dede" was my grandmothers nickname. Charles answered, "yes". So my father sent the yard boy to bring 2 horses and have them saddled. Then he and I went to Rambaud. He had to take care of all formalities for the evening wake and I to take care of the coffin. He remained there and I went back to town after having taken her measures as to make the right sized coffin.

I then contacted Mr. Adolphus Halley and had him furnish me the necessary material. Along with one of his sons I made the coffin which was ready about 11 o'clock in the morning. I transported it to Rambaud and started to make the preparations for the burial. I was very much criticized by some of the villagers because when the time came to close the coffin, after all of the family and friends had paid the last tribute to her, I placed the cover on and put the screws in place. At that moment many of the old ladies present called me a brute, saying that at my age of 16 years I was heartless.

I remember some other little events of that funeral. It was the custom that the entire population of the village had something as a farewell to the dead. A little girl by the name of Antoinette Manuel came forward and said, "So long Dede, oh I will miss you. Oh Dede you wont be there when I am passing in the morning and you are sitting by the window taking your coffee. I'd say to you, "Morning Dede", after I repeat it three times, you will answer, "Little girl, go, I'm eating now." Her death was a big loss for that village because it was at her home that all the children came together to learn the catechism, and even to read and write because many of the parents could not sent all their children to school in Marigot.

# Mini – Stories Of The Past
# By Paul Amedee Richardson

## Philippe, the St. Martin Lieutenant in World War I

My grandparents William Henry Richardson Jr. and Carron Baly had 5 sons and 4 daughters. Their youngest son was my uncle Phillippe Richardson. I would not mention him if there were not a few remarkable facts in his life.

I remember that his first wife, Estelle Dormoy, died very young in 1914. they had no children. Then he was drafted into the Army in 1914 and served for the entire 5 years of World War I. He had been to the Dardanellas for some time and sent back to France, where he was under the command of General Joffre, when he stopped the Germans at Verdun to prevent Paris from getting invaded.

At that time, being at the rank of Lieutenant, he was decorated for his bravery. After the Armistice in November 1918 (On St. Maarten's Day!!) the majority of the Antillean soldiers was sent back to their homes with a very good pension. So he returned to St. Martin in 1919, and in 1922 he got married again, this time to Dorese Hunt. She died in 1941, leaving him for the second time a widower. Again they had no children.

Philippe was a first class violinist, and he was playing the violin until his death in 1950.

A very special thanks to the granddaughter
of Paul Joseph Amedee Richardson,
Mrs. Judith Ras – Bickell.

## Antoine Richardson

## Raphael Richardson

## Ostend Richardson

## Hector Richardson

## Constance Richardson

## Jo-Jo, Yvonne, and Gaby Richardson

The last 2 remaining children of
Joseph Emanuel Richardson,
Neil Kruytoff and Carmen Carrington
– Neil Kruytoff is
The last child, number 67

# Richardson/Hughes/Baly/Barrington/Rovelet/Brooks/Family Origins

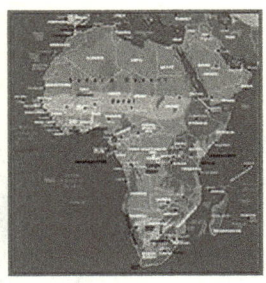

Africa

Ireland

The United Kingdom

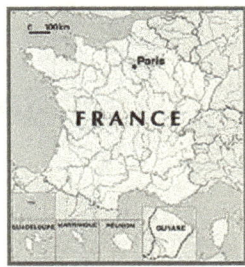

France

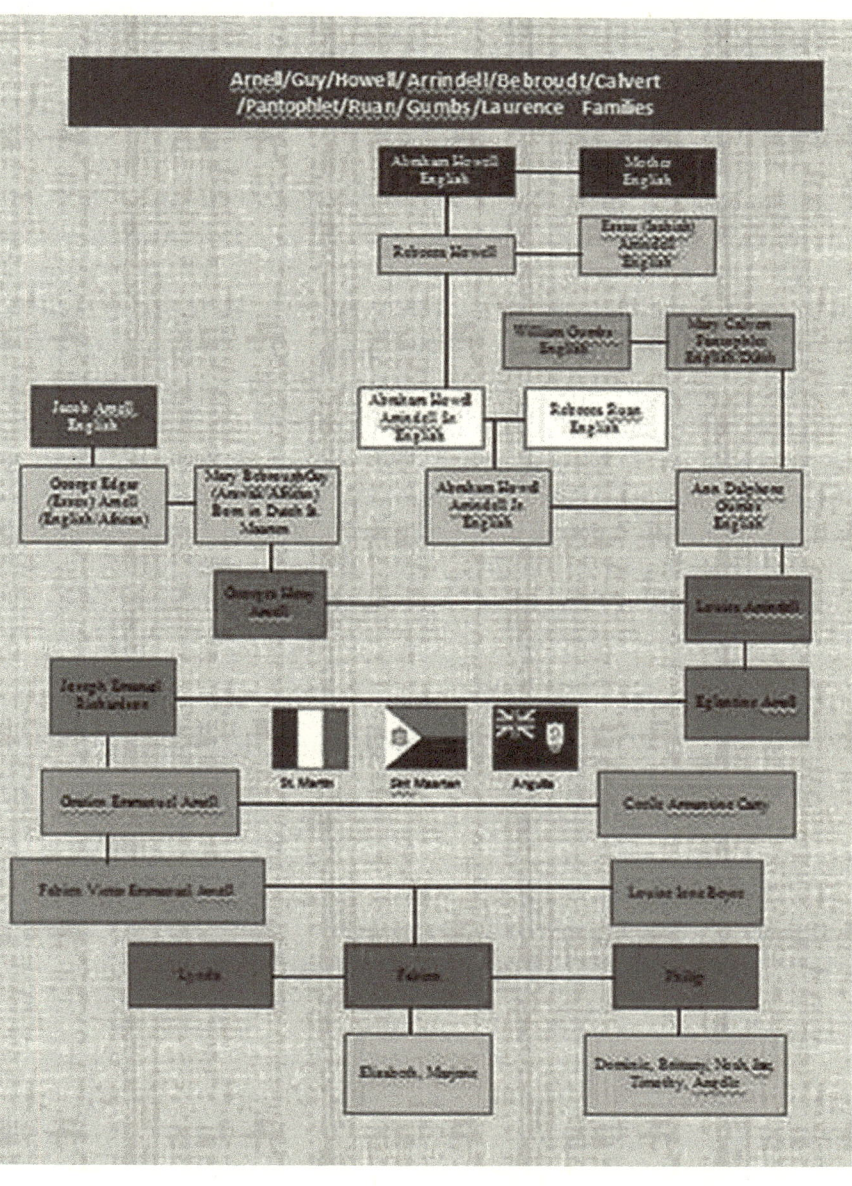

# THE ARNELL/GUY/HOWELL/ARRINDELL/BEBROUDT/CALVERT /PANTOPHLET/RUAN/GUMBS/LAURENCE FAMILIES OF ST. MAARTEN, NA /ST. MARTIN, FWI /ANGUILLA

### Parents:

**Georges Henry Arnell** (December 1, 1859 – January 21, 1931): Known as "Georgefoot" for being the "great outdoorsman always on the move". His family were the Guy's and Bebroudt's on his mother side (**Mary Ann Elizabeth Bebroudt (Bebrough**) and the Arnell's and the Gumbs from his father (**Essex Georges Edgar Arnell**). His lineage was a mixture of English, Amerindian (Arawak), and African. His occupation was a "jack of all trades" from carpentry to raising cattle. He and his father were born on the French side and his mother was from the Dutch side from the Guana Bay area located in the town of "Sucker Gardens" where they all resided in his youth. The original family name was of English extraction, Arrindell. Two names were spun off from this name. The French adaptation was "Arnell", the Dutch adaptation was "Andell". All one family.

Half Siblings – Marcellin Louis Arnell, Jean Adolphe Arnell, Marie Louise Arnell

### Georges Parents:

**Essex Georges Edgar Arnell** – born 1837
**Mary Ann Elizabeth Bebroudt (Bebrough)** – born 1843

### Essex Father:

**Jacob Arnell** – 1795 – 1860
Mother's name unknown

Anne Louisa Arrindell Arnell_(1859 – 1940) - Born in "French Quarter" Saint Martin". Known as "Grandmother Mona". Her Lineage was Celtic, Out of England and Ireland and French. Born on the French side of St. Martin. Family names: Arrindell/Ruan (father's family), Gumbs/Laurence/Calvert (mother's family). Her siblings: **Estine, Esther-Ann (Hessie), Caroline, Albert, Don, Robert Alexander, Edmund Luke, Ann Redella, Abraham Burke, Mary Margaret, Susanna Rebecca, Charles Louis.** Half Brother – Peter Gustave Arrindell

<u>Ann Louisa's Family:</u>

**Great – Great Grandfather – Abraham Howell (Birth Unknown – 1727)**

He was a British colonial Deputy Governor of Anguilla from 1666 to 1689. Official title: **Deputy Governor and Commander in Chief over all His Majesty's Forces, Officers and Soldiers in Anguilla.** Was instrumental in the settlement early Anguillians off of the small island off of Puerto Rico known now known as **Vieques**, originally known as "Crab Island".

**Great – Great Grandmother – name unknown, birth and death unknown**
**Great Grandmother – Rebecca Howell, birth and death unknown**
**Great Grandfather – Essau (Isahia) Arrindell, birth and death unknown**
**Grandfather - Abraham Howell Arrindell Sr. – born 1760, died 1824 St. Martin**
**Grandmother Rebecca Ruan – born 1772**

Abraham was born in Island Harbor, Anguilla and Rebecca was born in Sandy Hill, Anguilla. Both were children of indentured white servants then later moved to St. Martin FWI).

## Children of Abraham Howell Arrindell Sr & Rebecca Ruan:

Luke Arrindell – 1797-1872
America Arrindell - 1798
Adelaide Arrindell – 1814
Ann Arrindell – 1815
Abraham Howell Arrindell Jr. – 1816
Father – Abraham Howell Arrindell Jr. - born 1816
Mother - Ann Delphine Gumbs – Born 1826 – French Quarter

## Ann Delphine Gumbs Parents:

William Reran Gumbs – born 1801
Mary Calvert (fathers last name) - Pantophlet – born 1794
in Lancaster, England
Half Brother – John Richard Gumbs

## The Children of Georges and Anne Louisa Arnell

Joel Arnell
**Eglantine Arnell – Mother of 2 – Gratien and Marie**
Marie Elizabeth Arnell
Virginie Arnell
Royus Arnell
Jacques Adolphe
Henriette (Hennie) Arnell Vlaun – Mother of 21 children
Marta Arnell – Mother of 1 child
George Alexander (Zander) Arnell – Father of 1 child
James (Boo) Arnell
Guillaume Henri (Willie) Arnell – Father of 1 child
Urie Arnell
Susanne (Gussie) Arnell – Mother of 10 children
George Matinus Arnell – Father of 5 child
Anna Pauline Arnell
Agathe Constance Arnell
Baby Girl – Died after birth
Richard Bryan – ½ brother (George's Side)
Baby – ½ brother died after birth (George's Side)

**Eglantine Arnell (Nocco): Feb 21, 1884 – 1966.** She had two children with Joseph Emmanuel Richardson; Gratien Emmanuel ("Manin") 1905 - 1981, Marie 1912 - 1991. She was born in French Cul De Sac - Saint Martin. In later years after becoming blind she migrated to Tintamaire (Flat Island) off of French St. Martin then to the island of Aruba to live with her daughter Marie where she resided until her death in 1966.

Up until May of 1996, the sole survivors of this family were the last child of George and Louisa, Alexander (Zander), he was 96 years old, and in 1998, Richard Bryan (son of George), age unknown. The most recent surviving sibling before the last 2 was Marta who died in 1987. She was approximately 88 years old. This family exists throughout the world through a vast number of offspring.

**Family Names:**

**Arnell**
**Arrindell (all various spellings)**
**Howell**
**Andell**
**Gumbs**
**Bebroudt (Bebrough)**
**Guy**
**Calvert**
**Pantophlet**
**Ruan**
**Laurence**
Mingo
Thomas
Peterson
Flanders
Vlaun
Larmonie (all various spellings)

**\*Bold print means direct bloodline**

# Eglantine Arnell (Nocco)

## Susanne (Gussie) Arnell

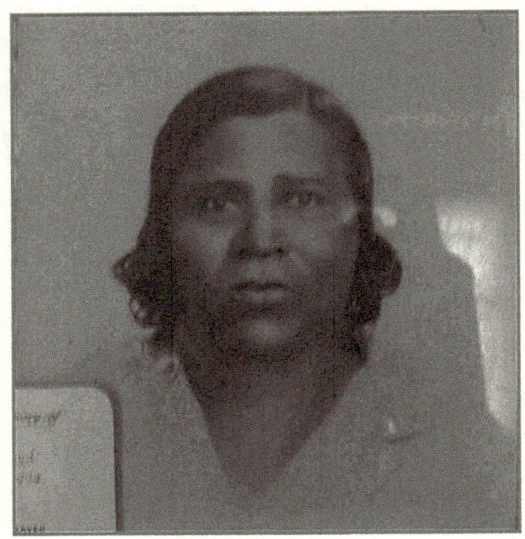

## George Matinus Arnell

## Anna Arnell

## Richard Bryan (Arnell)

# Marta Arnell

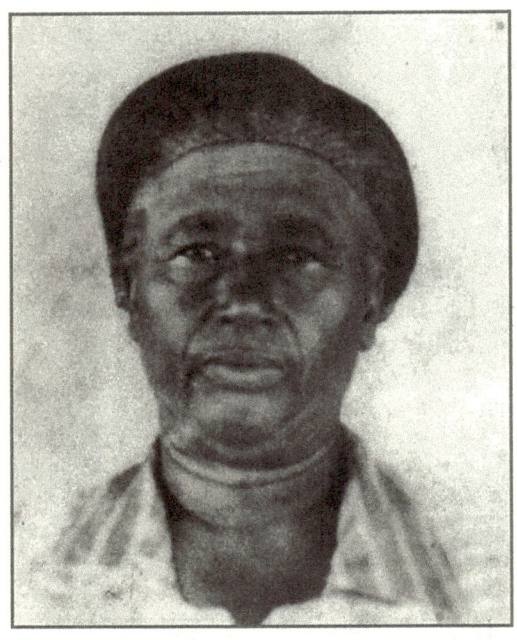

# Henrietta (Hennie) Arnell – Vlaun

## Guillaume (Willie) Henri Arnell

## George Alexander Arnell (Zander)

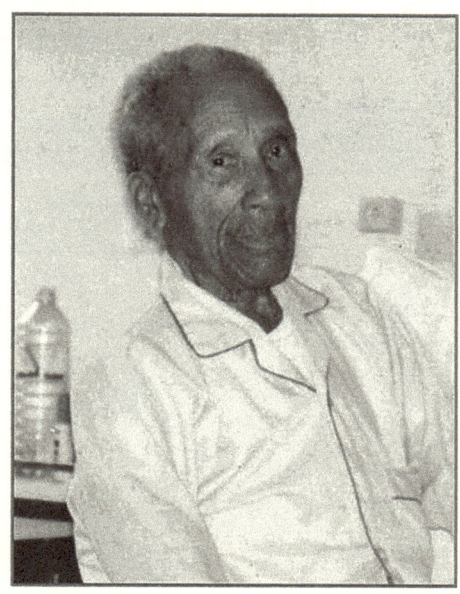

# The Original Arnell Family

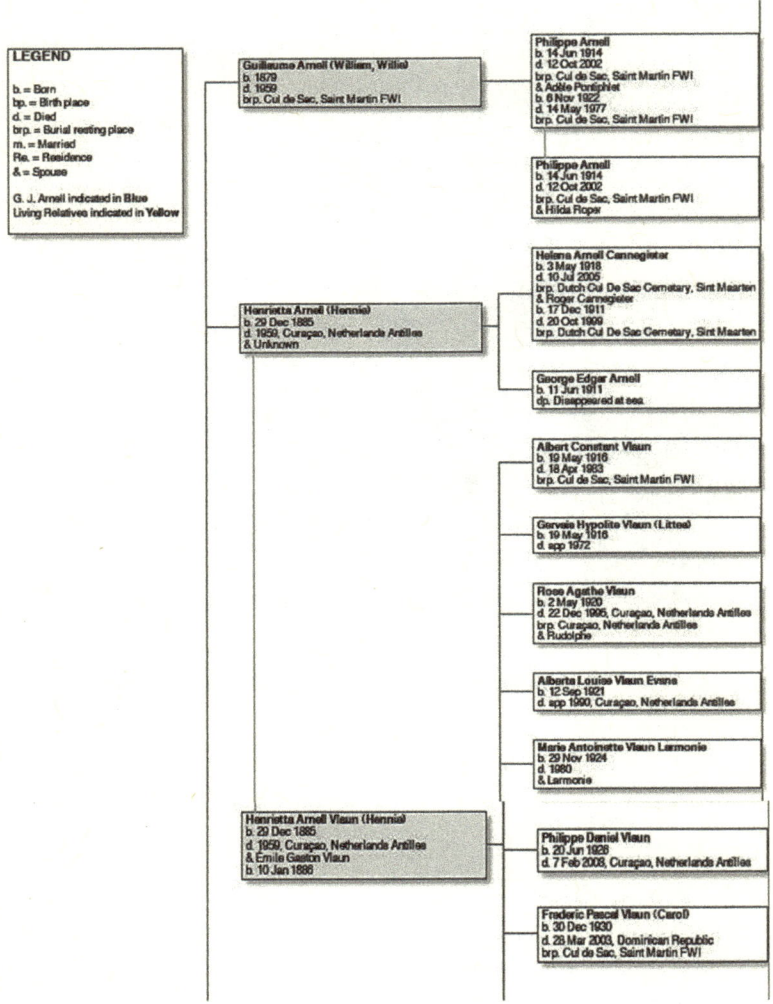

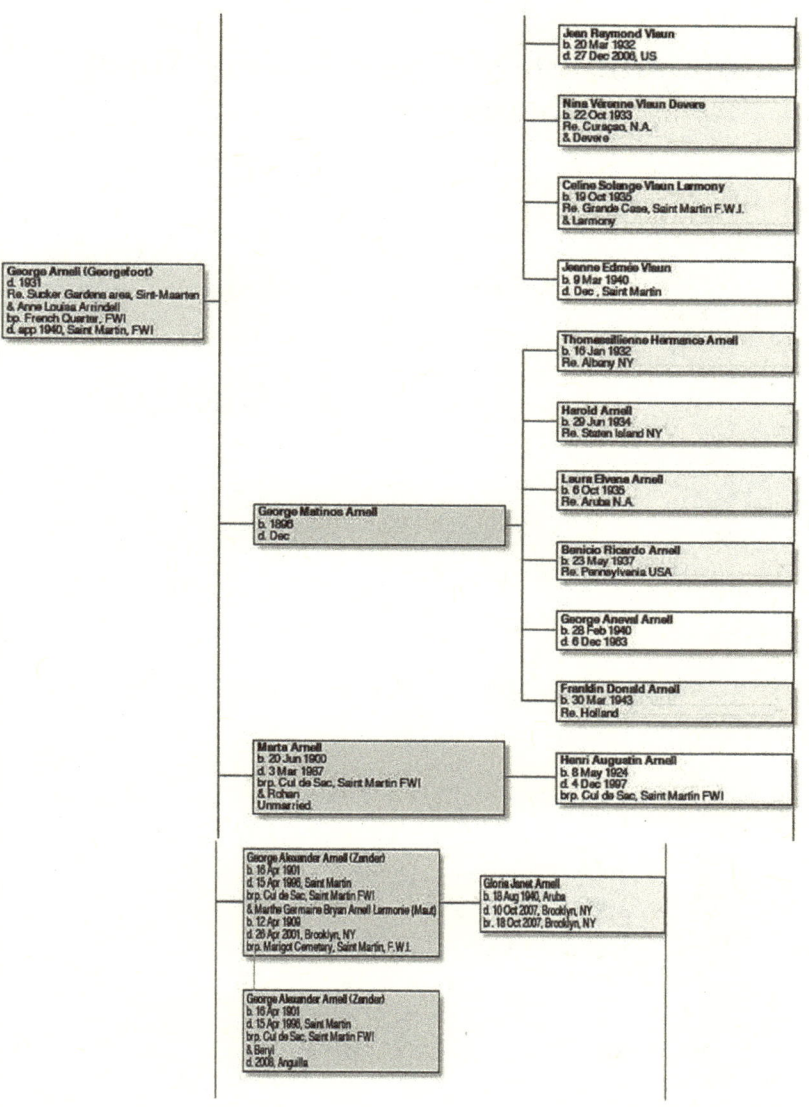

**Birth certificate of Georges Henry Arnell (Georgefoot)**

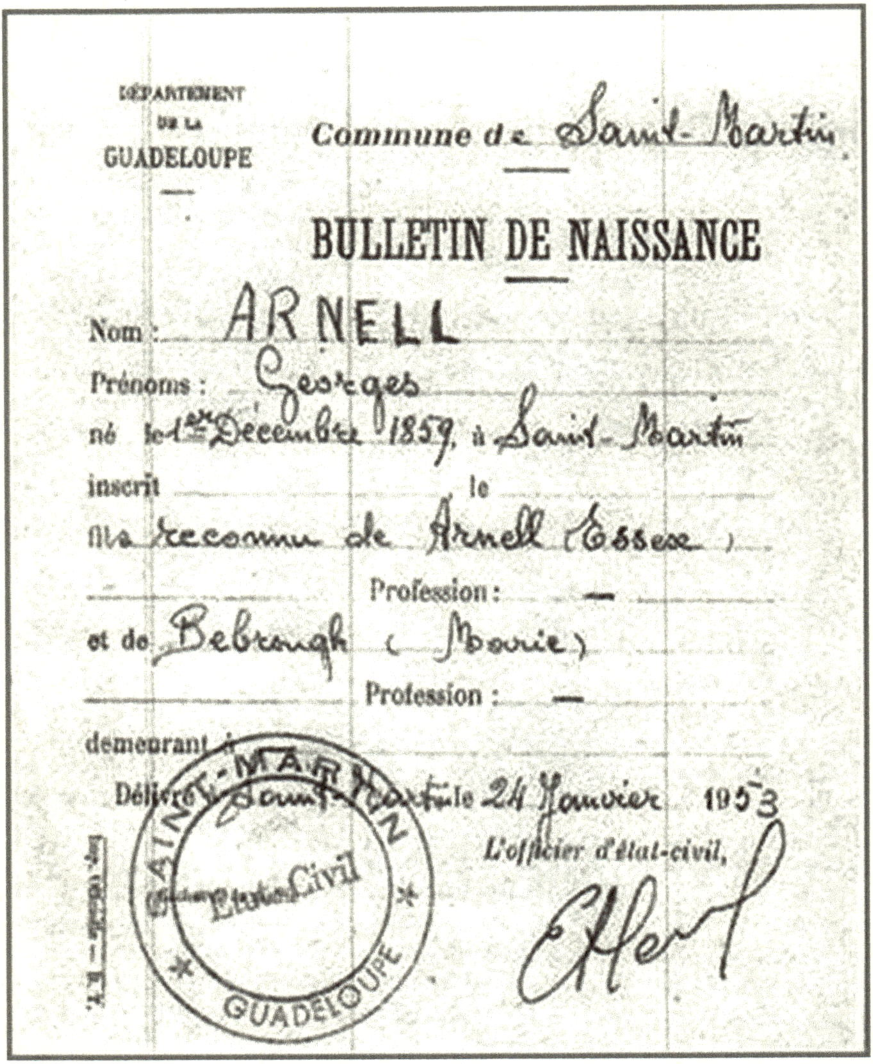

DÉPARTEMENT DE LA GUADELOUPE

Commune de Saint-Martin

BULLETIN DE NAISSANCE

Nom : ARNELL

Prénoms : Georges

né le 1er Décembre 1859, à Saint-Martin

inscrit le

fils reconnu de Arnell (Essex),

Profession : —

et de Bebrough (Marie)

Profession : —

demeurant à

Délivré à Saint-Martin le 24 Janvier 1953

L'officier d'état-civil,

SAINT-MARTIN GUADELOUPE

État Civil

# Death certificate of Georges Henry Arnell (Georgefoot)

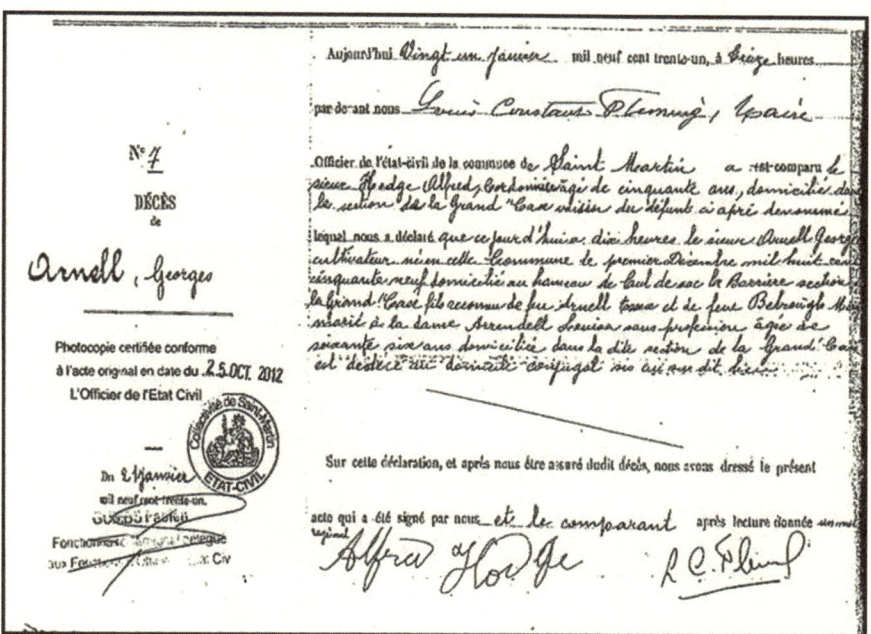

# Arnell/Guy/Arrindell/Howell/Bebrough/Gumbs/Pantophlet/Ruan/Laurence Family Origins

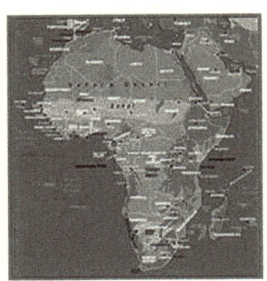

Africa

South America

Ireland

The Netherlands

The United Kingdom

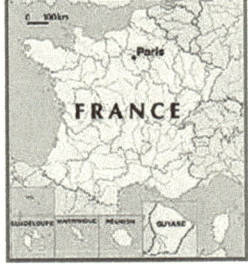

France

# Children of Joseph Richardson and Eglantine Arnell

### Gratien Emmanuel Arnell: 1905 – 1981

A Master Carpenter for his time. Schooled in Guadeloupe and in the Dominican Republic. Much of his work still stands strong in St. Maarten, St. Martin, Anguilla, Aruba, Curacao, Guadeloupe, Dominican Republic, and a variety of other places. He married Cecile Armantine Carty of Anguilla in 1930. He was the father of eight children, Armantine and Jeanne from a prior relationship. Together with Armantine they had Maria, Rodrique, Fabien, Nicholas, Armelle, and Cassie. He passed away on March 11, 1981 at the age of 75 in Queens, New York. The family lives on throughout the world generation after generation due to their vast amount of offspring.

### Marie Arnell : 1912 – 1991

A homemaker. A master cook, well known for her apple pies. She arrived in Aruba in 1938 and married Wilhelmus Alias. Together they raised 3 children, Donna, Kenneth, and Kathy, and had 15 grandchildren. She passed away in Aruba on August 15, 1991 at the age of 79.

# The Birth Cerificate of
## Gratien Emmanuel (Mannin)Arnell

# Gratien Emmanuel Arnell (Mannin)

# Cistern of Mannin Arnell.
# It is still in working use today.
# Dated May 16, 1931

## Marie Arnell - Alias

# The Arnell Family Church
# Mary Star of the Sea
# Grand Case, St. Martin, FWI

# Countries to Where the Families Have Spread

| | |
|---|---|
| United States | Haiti |
| United Kingdom | Cuba |
| Switzerland | St. Kitts |
| France | Nevis |
| The Netherlands | Martinique |
| Venezuela | Guadeloupe |
| St. Thomas | St. Croix |
| Aruba | St. Eustasius |
| Bonaire | St. Barthelemy |
| Curacao | Saba |
| Dominican Republic | Dominica |
| St. Lucia | Antigua |
| St. Vincent | Montserrat |
| Puerto Rico | Suriname |
| Canada | Australia |

# The Arnell Family

## Gratien and Armantine Arnell - Married 1930

# For the Offsprings of Gratien and Armantine Arnell....

**Cistern** - a waterproof receptacle for holding liquids, usually water. Cisterns are often built to catch and store rainwater. Cisterns are distinguished from wells by their waterproof linings. Modern cisterns range in capacity from a few liters to thousands of cubic meters, effectively forming covered reservoirs.

This is a very special page. This is a cistern that was built in 1929 in Anguilla. Gratien E. Arnell (Mannin) was commissioned by Margaret Eliza Hodge Carty (Grandsall) to build this cistern in front of her house. On this very job he met Margaret's daughter, Cecile Armantine Carty. On March 30th, 1930, they became husband and wife and they had a family together. Without this one job, Gratien and Armantine would most likely would have never met. Without this one job, none of their children together would have been born, and the same for their future generations up to the present day. This cistern was in full working order up until the mid 2000's, providing water for all who wished to draw from it. It was a pillar of the community for so many years, thanks to Mannin's master craftsmanship. Unfortunately the cistern is no longer in existence. Thanks to cousin Devern Flemming, we have a picture of this family treasure that surely represents, "From Whence We Came, to Where We Continue."

# Marriage Certificate of Gratien and Armantine Arnell

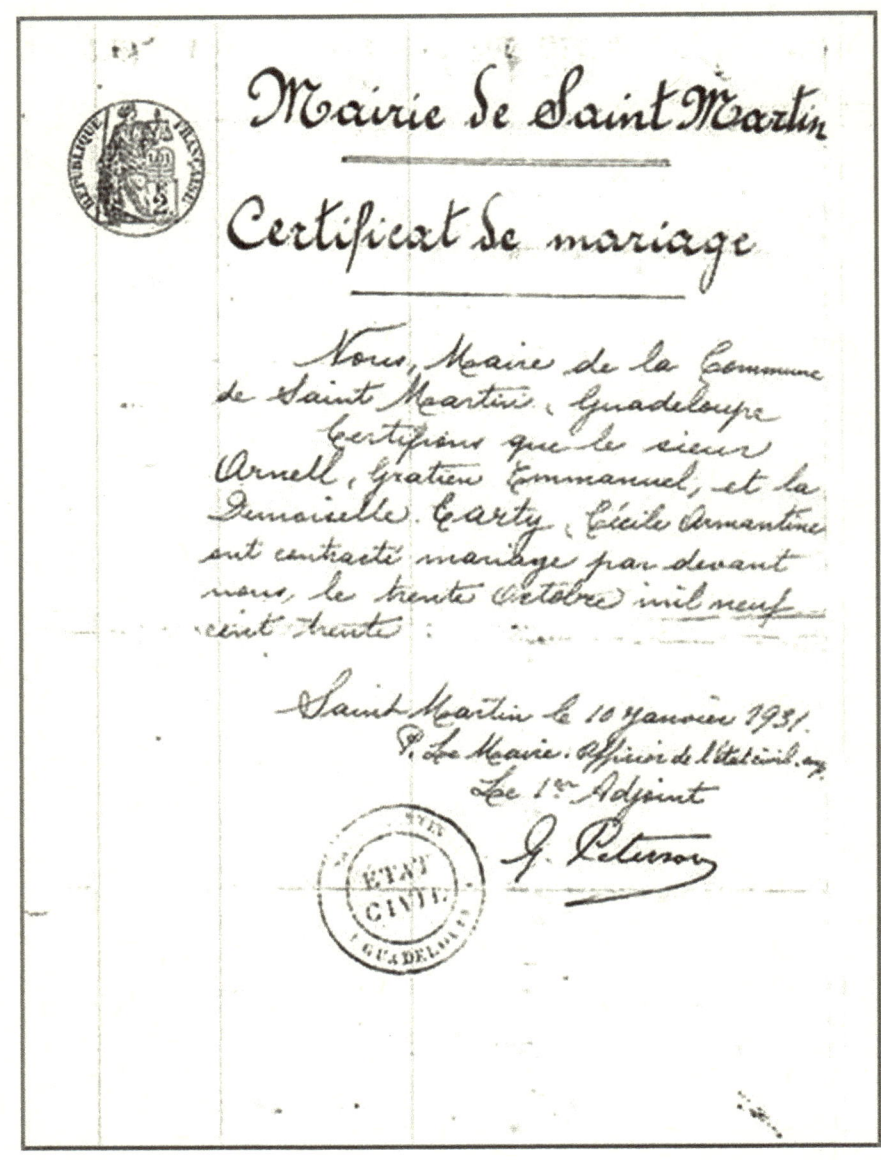

**For Gratien and Helen Smith**

# Armentine Susanna Laurence 1928 – 2010
## (Monty)

# Jeanne Elfrida Laurence Brill  1930 - 2008

For Gratien and Armantine

Maria Arnell –  B - 1932- D - 1932  - 3 days old

# Gratien Rodrique Arnell (Rico)

# Fabien Victor Emmanuel

# Eustache Nicholas Arnell

## The 3 Musketeers – 1939
## Fabien age 4, Nicholas age 3, Rico age 5

# Armelle Elpinesse Arnell

# Cassie Rhea Arnell

# ARNELL FAMILY MIGRATION

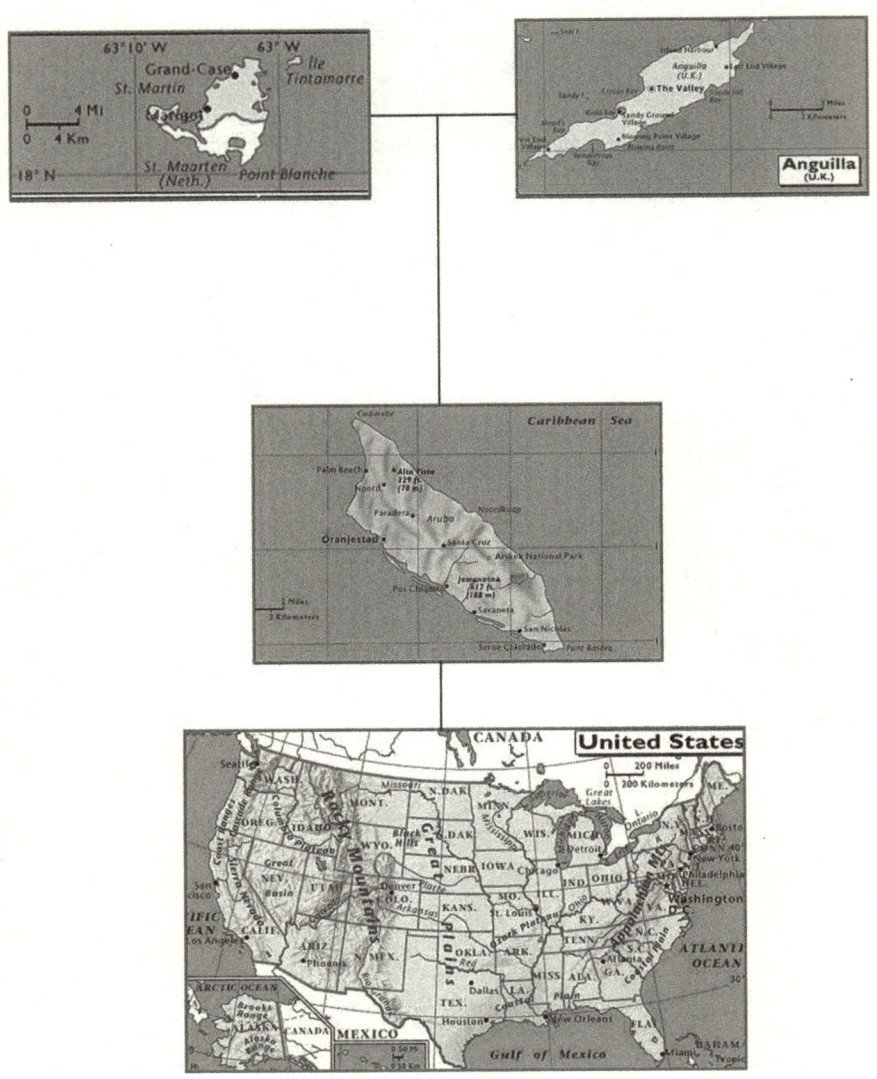

From St. Martin and Anguilla to Aruba finally
settling in The United States

# The Children in More Recent Years

The final family photo with
Armantine and children

# The Remaining Siblings Today

## Mr. & Mrs. Gratien & Armantine Arnell

# Final Resting Place of Gratien and Cecile Arnell – Pinelawn Memorial Cemetary – Melville, NY

# The Generations That Follow.....

# The Children's Children, and So on............

## Armentine Susanna (Monty)

**Melsadice** (Sadie) (deceased) - 2 Children – Dougie, Josianne
Grandchildren – Erica, Krizia, Kemo
Great grandchildren – Katara, Kaiden
**Patsy** (deceased) – No Children
**Marvio** (Kleen) (deceased) - 7 Children - Marvio, Marvia, plus 5 children
Grandchildren – Sharell, Tyrell, Jairo, plus 8 others
**Sandra** - 2 -Children – Omar and Amir
**Glenford** – 11- Children - Jackie, Vincenzia, Glenford, plus 8 others
Grandchildren – Zion, Mason
**Yolanda** (Yolie) (deceased) – No Children
**Ascencio** (deceased) - 1- Child - Jaire
**Nilda** - 4 - Children – Edouard, Rodrique, Guillume, Raquel
Grandchildren - Xaina, Keryna, Etaisha, Jaykwon
**Lester** (deceased) – 3 - Children – Gregory, Wendell, Wendelica
Grandchildren - Reina
**Erno** (Terry) (deceased) – 2- Children – Erno, Raisha
**Hencio** (Ricky) – No Children

**Maria** -

## Jeanne Elfrida

**Glenda** – No Children
**Rudolf (Dolphy)** (deceased)
7 Children – Angelique, Jamal, Angelo, Amy, Elijah, Plus 2
Grandchild - Zahrius
**Charles (Charley)** - 2 Children – Charlisca, Jomarly
**Daphnie** – (deceased) – No Children
**Norma** – No Children
**Louise** - 1Child - Loudahlia
**Leana** - 1Child - Aneeka
**Swinda** – No Children

## Gratien Rodrique (Rico)

**Jose** - Children – Damien, Scottie, Naomi
Grandchildren - Scottie Jr.
**Laura** - 3 Children - Rita, Edgar, Brandon
Grandchildren – Samantha, Zachary, Quentin, Brandon Jr.
**Casta** – 1 Child - Devon
**Rosa** - 3 Children – Quincey, Iris, Shane
**Arlene**
Children - Meghan Rose, Madison

## Fabien Victor Emmanuel

**Lynda** – No Children
**Pierre**
Children – Elisabeth, Marjorie
**Philip (Tim)**
Children – Dominic, Brittany, Noah, Jase, Timothy, Angelle

## Eustache Nicholas

**Camille** – No Children
**Donna** – 3 Children – Sean (1 child), Marisa (1 child), Aleena
**Elaine** – 1 Child – Arielle
**Nicholas** – 2 Children – Joi – Elle, Jon Aaron
**Yolanda** – 2 Children – Sacha (1 child), Joshua
**Nicole** – No children

## Armelle Elpinesse

**Tania -** 2 Children - Imani, Mirai, Camila, Marcus
**Evan –** 1 Child - Elena
**Marc -** 1Child - Issac

## Cassie Rhea

**Robert**
Children – Dorian, Desiree, Robert, Leonardo
Grandchildren – 1 Grandson
**Doreen**
Children - Matthew
**Desiree**
Children -Ivan, Richard, Nicolette

## TOTAL

 8 Children
39 Grand-children
83 Great- Grand Children
13 Great - Great Grand Children
 2 Great Great Great Grandchildren

**and STILL counting………………...**

# First Cousins, What Number Grandchild Are You?

1) Melsadice (Sadie)
2) Patsy
3) Marvio
4) Sandra
5) Glenda
6) Dolphy
7) Glenford
8) Yolanda
9) Charles
10) Jose
11) Laura
12) Daphne
13) Ascencio
14) Norma
15) Camille
16) Donna
17) Nilda
18) Lynda
19) Robert
20) Louise
21) Elaine
22) Lester
23) Casta
24) Nicholas
25) Rosa
26) Doreen
27) Desiree
28) Pierre
29) Leana
30) Erno
31) Yolanda
32) Sweenda
33) Tania
34) Philip (Tim)
35) Evan
36) Marc
37) Hencio
38) Nicole
39) Arlene

## Grandkids and so on……….

**Fabien and Louise Arnell
Married May 17, 1958**

## Mr. and Mrs. Philip and Paula Arnell

Tim's kids – Dominic, Brittany, Noah, Jase, Timothy, and Cassidy

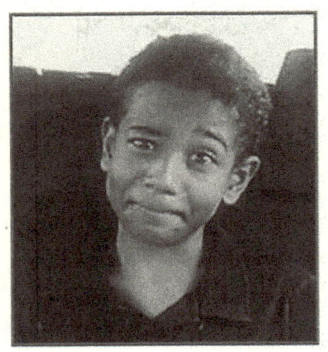
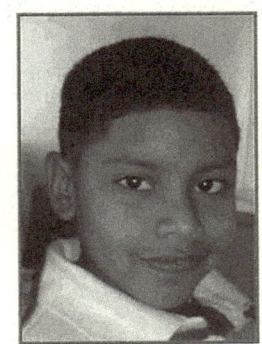
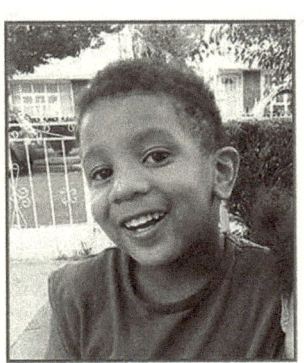

# Tim's family

## Fabien's son Pierre

## Monty with Fabien's grandchildren Brittany and Noah

Rico with Arlene

Armelle with Marc, Tania, and Evan

**Fabien with grandchildren Noah and Brittany**

Jeanne with grandchildren
Elijah, Amy and Loudahlia

**Monty's grandson Marvio with wife Ashlye**

### Jeanne's granddaughter Aneeka and daughter Leana

## Monty's sons Glenford and Ricky

Nicholas's grandson Joshua

Nicholas's daughter Donna
with children Aleena, Sean, and Marissa

## Jeanne's daughter Norma

# Monty's daughter Sandra

# Jeanne's grandson Jamal

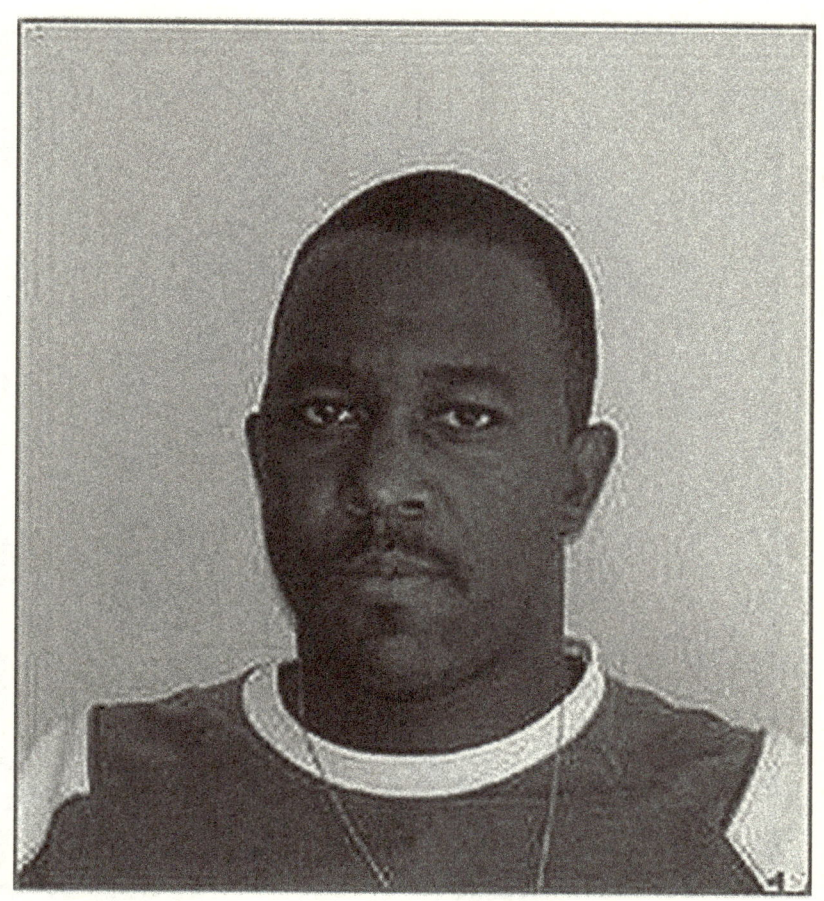

# Jeanne's granddaughter Angelique

Nicholas's son Nicholas

Nicholas's daughter Yolanda and granddaughter Joi-Elle

**Casta with husband John and daughter Devon**

**Rico's daughter Arlene with Husband Kevin and daughters Meghan and Madison**

## Cassie's son Robert

## Nicholas's daughter Elaine

## Monty's granddaughter Gilma

## Monty's grandson Eddy

Monty's granddaughter Raquel

## Jeanne's daughter Louise

Jeanne's daughter Sweenda with husband Fabian

Monty's great - granddaughter Erica

## Monty's grandson's Amir and Omar

## Monty's granddaughter Josieanne

## Jeanne's granddaughter Amy

## Jeanne's grandson Elijah

Monty's great - granddaughter Krizia

## Monty's grandson Gregory

## Monty's granddaughter Marvia

## Monty's daughter Nilda

## Jeanne's granddaughter Charlisca

## Jeanne's daughter Glenda

## Jeanne's son Charlie

Jeanne's grandson Angelo with his wife
Marcheena and son Zahrius

## Monty's grandson Guillaume

Rico's daughter Rosa with her children Shane, Iris, and Quincey

### Rico's children – Jose, Laura, Casta, Rosa, and Arlene

## Nick's granddaughter Sacha

## Armelle's granddaughter Elena

Many have asked through the years when they have learned about their families, how they and everyone else were connected. This chart has been made to answer those questions. Read from column number one vertically with column number one horizontally to find your connections.

## Cousins Chart

| Generations | 1 | 2 | 3 | 4 | 5 | 6 | 7 | 8 | 9 | 10 |
|---|---|---|---|---|---|---|---|---|---|---|
| 1 | Common Ancestor: ie Mother or father | Son or Daughter | Grandson or daughter | Great-Grandson or daughter | 2nd Great-Grandson or daughter | 3rd Great-Grandson or daughter | 4th Great-Grandson or daughter | 5th Great-Grandson or daughter | 6th Great-Grandson or daughter | 7th Great-Grandson or daughter |
| 2 | Son or Daughter | Siblings (brother or sister) | nephew or niece | Great-Great nephew or niece | 2nd Great nephew or niece | 3rd Great nephew or niece | 4th Great nephew or niece | 5th Great nephew or niece | 6th Great nephew or niece | 7th Great nephew or niece |
| 3 | Grandson or Daughter | Nephew or niece | First Cousin | First Cousin once removed | First Cousin twice removed | First Cousin 3 times removed | First Cousin 4 times removed | First Cousin 5 times removed | First Cousin 6 times removed | First Cousin 7 times removed |
| 4 | Great Grandson or Daughter | Grand Nephew or Niece | First cousin once Removed | Second Cousin | Second Cousin once Removed | Second Cousin 3 times Removed | Second Cousin 4 times Removed | Second Cousin 5 times Removed | Second Cousin 6 times Removed | Second Cousin seven times Removed |
| 5 | 2nd Great Grandson or Daughter | Great Grand Nephew or niece | First cousin twice Removed | Second Cousin once Removed | Third Cousin | Third Cousin once removed | Third Cousin twice removed | Third Cousin 3 times removed | Third Cousin 4 times removed | Third Cousin 5 times removed |
| 6 | 3rd Great Grandson or Daughter | 2nd Great Grand Nephew or niece | First cousin 3 times Removed | Second Cousin twice Removed | Third Cousin once Removed | Fourth Cousin | Fourth Cousin once Removed | Fourth Cousin twice Removed | Fourth Cousin 3 times Removed | Fourth Cousin 4 times Removed |
| 7 | 4th Great Grandson or Daughter | 3rd Great Grand Nephew or niece | First cousin 4 times Removed | Second Cousin 3 times removed Removed | Third Cousin twice Removed | Fourth Cousin once Removed | Fifth Cousin | Fifth Cousin once Removed | Fifth Cousin twice removed | Fifth cousin 3 times removed |
| 8 | 5th Great Grandson or Daughter | 4th Great Grand Nephew or niece | First cousin 5 times Removed | Second Cousin 4 times Removed | Third Cousin 3 times Removed | Fourth Cousin twice Removed | Fifth Cousin once Removed | Sixth Cousin | Sixth Cousin once Removed | Sixth Cosuin Twice Removed |
| 9 | 6th Great Grandson or Daughter | 5th Great Grand Nephew or niece | First cousin 6 times Removed | Second Cousin 5 times Removed | Third Cousin 4 times Removed | Fourth Cousin 3 times Removed | Fifth Cousin twice removed | Sixth Cousin once Removed | Seventh Cousin | Seventh Cousin Once Removed |
| 10 | 7th Great Grandson or Daughter | 6th Great Grand Nephew or niece | First cousin seven Removed | Second Cousin 6 times Removed | Third Cousin 5 times Removed | Fourth Cousin 4 times Removed | Fifth cousin 3 times removed | Sixth Cousin Twice Removed | Seventh Cousin Once Removed | Eighth Cousin |

# IN MEMORIUM

Yolanda Laurence
1956-1963

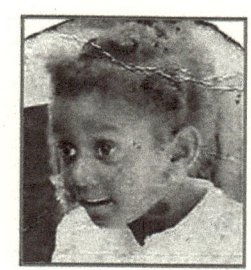

Dorita Melsadice Laurence
(Sadie)
1945-2001

Lester Wendell Laurence
1963-1991

Erno Terrell Richardson
1966-2001

Rudolph Elmando Brill
1955 -2001

Daphnie Darlene Brill
1959-1988

Jeanne Elfrida
Laurence - Brill
1930-2008

Ascencio Ishmael Davis
1958-2009

Armentine Susanna
Laurence (Monty)
1928-2010

**Marvio Esperanzo Laurence
(Kleen)
1951-2012**

We Miss You, and Love You All......

# Fortunate Member Of A Caribbean Diaspora

# Fortunate Member of a Caribbean Diaspora

*Diaspora: a dispersion of a people, language, or culture that was formerly concentrated in one place.*

Some 34 years ago, I began a project documenting the history of my family. It actually started in March 1981 when I was just 12 years old. Shortly after my grandfather Gratien Emmanuel (Mannin) Arnell passed away, while visiting with my grandmother Cecile Armantine Carty-Arnell, I started to ask questions about the family. I was amazed at the things that she told me: who my ancestors were; what they did; and how they lived their lives. The more questions I asked, the more information I received. I remember her saying to me, "Make a record of this information so that it won't be forgotten." I took her words to heart. From then, as an inquisitive 12 year old up until the present, I have gathered information about my family's history. I have visited the various islands connected to my family countless times to the point that they have become an extension of my own home.

I have had the esteemed pleasure of meeting and interviewing relatives who lived from those "near-forgotten times" and who provided me treasures of knowledge about my culture(s). Why did it take all of 34 years? Firstly, I wasn't able to travel by myself until I was an adult. Secondly, all works of passion need time to grow and mature. Thirdly, the advent of the internet has contributed to the growth of my family log by allowing me to publish it online and thereby establish contacts which would have been otherwise impossible, and it has facilitated my research. I am convinced that now is the best time to present this body of work to the world.

When I was 13, I visited St. Maarten/St. Martin and Anguilla for the first time with my parents (Fabien and Louise Arnell) and siblings (Lynda and Pierre). I was fortunate enough to learn quite a bit about the culture(s) of my family from both of my parents, and to be raised in that culture. My mother (Louise Ione Boyce-Arnell) is a Barbadian American. I have visited Barbados a number of times as well. In our home it was almost like being raised in the Caribbean. All that was really missing was the warm weather and blue water and white sand beaches year-round. When you went outside of the home, you were in America. I know many Caribbean Diaspora children who have said the same. It is very true. Some will argue, "How can you say that? You are not actually there, you live someplace else." My proven factual argument is, "I wasn't raised in the street or in someone else's home by strangers from this country. I was raised in my home by my parents and grandparents...prove me wrong." Your way of life is the culture you were raised in and that was practiced at home. You take it with you when you go out, and you will be smart to remember to practice it in the way you carry yourself...or else!

For all of us, it was a wonderful experience to go and see where our father and the rest of his family were from. We met his sisters and their children, dozens of cousins and saw where our forefathers lived. From that first experience, we bonded with our newfound family and relatives that we had been separated from for many years. Some of these were persons whose existence we had not previously been aware of. The best part is that we have maintained our family ties and friendships with them to this very day, despite originally being separated for many years. I now know many of them better than other relatives here in the United

States. I have grown with them, had fun with them, and mourned for them when their time was up. I embrace my family because they are the reminders of who I am and who I was raised to be.

As the years came and went, I researched the family through interviews and records. I was fortunate enough to have had relatives who lived very long lives and kept their faculties about them so that they could provide me with whatever information I was looking for. I enjoyed my time with them though, for some, it was limited. It was an honor to visit numerous times, and sit and chat with them. Instantly they remembered me and continued with our conversations as if no time had passed since the last visit.

From this work, I have come to the realization that it has reunited and acquainted many generations of a family: live contacts with the living; as well as posthumous reunions through the offspring of immediate families. Some thought they would never see a picture of that person who they either lived amongst or became an offspring of. Finding a member of one's family from a branch that has spread out to different parts of the globe has been an extremely pleasant surprise. As copies of this work have been passed along through the years, I have been able to meet and establish relationships with relatives globally who were gracious enough to provide me with information, records, and pictures. By meeting them I have been able to learn more about myself.

One of my greatest accomplishments was reuniting with the grandchildren of my grandmother's brother, Aise Viotee Carty. His side of the family seemed to have disappeared from about the early 1980's. We knew he had children. He died in 1968 and his children died untimely deaths in the years following. We didn't know his grandchildren, we didn't know whether he had any. One day in 2012, I received a call from Lisa Carty-McNell. Lisa had seen my history log online. She asked for me, I accepted the call. Her first question was, "Have you ever heard of a man by the name of Aise Carty?" Instantly I knew this was a family member calling me. I had become very excited but had to maintain my composure due to the fact that I was at work. I told her I had heard of him and gave her some facts that I knew from the stories that I had been told through the years. I excused myself from the phone call to find a private area where I could speak with her. Once I went into a conference room, you could hear the excitement in my voice! My first words were, "OMG! Hey Gyirl! Cuz how you doin??"- a far cry from the composed professional business tone and jargon I had used in our prior conversation a few minutes earlier! She was completely overwhelmed with the emotions and significance of the moment. I learned that this was to be her last attempt to find her grandfather. If she didn't find him, that would be the end of it. She had "googled" his name, and lo and behold, it had popped up in connection with my name and my book!

She had no idea how large an immediate family her grandfather had come from (he was the last of 12 children), and how exorbitantly large his family is to this day. She had visited Anguilla some years before and had gone to the Records Office and found some information, but not a lot due to the limited time available. When she connected with me, I had the pleasure of connecting her with her roots that she knew very little of, as well as other off springs of her grandfather that she never knew she had. Lisa likes to go to St. Thomas. One of Great Uncle Aise's granddaughters has lived there for many years. Lisa has visited the island numerous times through the years, but had no idea that she had many cousins from her Anguillan connection living in St. Thomas. I connected the 2 granddaughters, and a long awaited relationship started. For all they knew, they could have passed each other a number of times, perhaps even said hello. I had the pleasure of meeting Lisa and her siblings when they made a special trip from Atlanta, Georgia to my home in New York. We have become very close since.

Another amazing story of meeting family occurred in June 2011. I had the pleasure of meeting Simone Boyd from the Arnell side of my family. I was going through my emails in the junk folder one day and saw her email. I read it and immediately knew who she was. Her grandfather's name was also Philip Arnell, and I had met him when I was 13. She wanted to find his obituary online and ended up finding my book which led her to me. She contacted me and introduced herself. She had no idea that she would have found the information that she did and all the familiar faces and names that she saw in this book. I have had the pleasure of establishing a close relationship with Simone as well. Meeting relatives that have the same passion as I do for finding their roots and for family overall builds the strongest relationships. I am grateful to have met them and to have them as a part of my life.

Another important story out of all of the family reconnections I have made was when I visited Anguilla in 1994. This trip was pivotal in my research of this book. I met my cousin Blondell Rodgiers for the first time and she led me to meet my grandmother's nieces and nephews. It was purely a case of being at the right place at the right time. I was in The Valley and passed an area where, on a prior trip, I had met a woman from who worked in an insurance company. I stopped in to visit but went into the wrong office. There was Blondell on the phone and she asked me to wait. When she finished the call she asked how could she help me. I told her I was looking for a lady whose last name was "Gumbs" and I just wanted to drop in and say hello since I was visiting. Needless to say, the person I was originally looking for wasn't in that office. As I continued to speak with Blondell, she asked the general questions, "where are you from?" etc. I told her a little about myself and that my grandmother was from Anguilla. She asked her name and I said, "Armantine Carty". She said, "Hmm, I believe my husband's mother has an aunt in the States named Armantine Carty, but I believe they call her Aunt Minnie."

She asked me if I knew someone named Armelle. I smiled and I said, "Armelle with the red hair and the freckles? She is my aunt and my grandmother's daughter". The connection had been made. Blondell gave me the names of my grandmother's nieces and nephews who lived in Island Harbor. I instantly sought them out and made my connections. To my surprise, some of them were persons I had already met on prior trips. Ironically those who I had met before said they knew I was their family by looking at me but they too didn't know exactly how I was related to them. I was very appreciative that they embraced and welcomed me the way they did since I was almost a total stranger.

When I returned to New York, I visited my grandmother with a great deal to tell her. I told her about the trip, and surprised her with pictures of her nieces and nephews whom she had had a hand in raising. Of course they had aged significantly but were still recognizable to her (in 1994) even though she had not seen nor heard from them since 1946, when she had moved first to Aruba and then in 1955 to New York. There had been some contact through common connections, but that was not a regular occurrence. It was wonderful to see her face light up and have endearing memories of them. She was of course too old to travel, and many of the relatives were too old as well, but they were now able to keep contact with each other, through my help, in their last years.

From that point on I kept meeting relatives though the years, establishing strong relationships, and learning of all of the multiple connections. In addition to acquiring so much research materials for my project from 1981 to 2001, I acquired a great deal of information in regard to the history of my family including pages of notes, pictures, etc. Finally it was time to compile everything into one uniform document. It started out to be 16 pages. It grew from there, in less than 2 years going to 60 pages, then to 80 pages then until recently close to 200 pages of information and pictures. I was very lucky to have been able to acquire all that I had in the early years because the relatives lived so long. They were able to give firsthand accounts of the information being searched for. My relatives were more accurate than records that were in archives. In today's world, technology has advanced so much that there are the internet and family research sites. They are very useful if your family is listed. Only in recent years have I turned to those sites when I wanted to get records or just to see what I could find.

It is a great feeling to know that you can connect with your roots. The customs and culture you grew up with now had faces to match the names of people, learned principles and endearing stories. I love the fact that from meeting the family through the years I was amazed as to how similar we were, simply by the way we were raised. The only differences were locations. Though location does play a role to some degree, the immediate principles were not lost once someone was moved from that environment. Reuniting people is not an easy task, but it is so rewarding when you give someone a picture of their father whom they had not seen in the flesh or in a picture since 1940, when he died. That is something very special, and unforgettable.

I remember important stories that I am privileged to share. One story was when my father (Fabien Victor Emmanuel Arnell) was reconnected with his sister Armantine Susanna Laurence, affectionately known as "Monty". When my Grandfather passed in 1981, all were notified. On the day of his burial, a woman whom we had never seen before appeared at the gravesite. The resemblance to my Grandfather was uncanny. Literally... it was him in a dress. She disappeared after the burial so no one knew who she was. Hours later she appeared at the house. When she walked in, my father looked at her and said "Monty!" And they gave each other an endearing hug. He said, "This is my sister!" We were quite taken back by his statement. We thought, "hmm, Dad's under a lot of stress, he thinks this woman is his sister". But fortunately he had all his wits about him and indeed this was his sister.

We just never heard about her, nor of their other sister Jeanne Elfrida Laurence - Brill. For some reason they were never spoken of. Monty and Jeanne were my grandfather's children from a prior relationship, respectfully. My grandfather had contact with them through the years, but simply no one spoke of them. They had not seen each other in almost 30 years. It was a touching reunion despite the circumstances. From that point on, we began meeting our first cousins from those two sisters and we have established close relationships with them through the years.

Another story was when we met my father's sister Jeanne Elfrida Laurence-Brill. Plans were made to visit St. Maarten/St. Martin in the summer of 1982. Just before this, my father had reached out to Jeanne by phone. She was overwhelmed with emotion since she had not seen nor spoken to her brother since 1946 when he had left St. Martin, FWI for Aruba, 36 years prior. Jeanne had never lived in Aruba, Monty on the other hand had done so for a number of years. My father, in order to keep the surprise, never let on to Jeanne that we were going to visit her.

Between March 1981 and August 1982 we had met with Monty, some of her kids, and 4 of Jeanne's children when they visited New York and began to get acquainted from there. This made the well-thought-out plan to surprise both sisters easier to execute because we had help.

August 17th, 1982 finally arrived. My parents and siblings and I went to St. Maarten/St. Martin. We arrived at the airport in the evening, and were greeted by many of our first cousins. We went to dinner and got acquainted with all those whom we had not yet met before that night. Finally we went off to see Monty and Jeanne. First we stopped at Monty, indeed a wonderful surprise for her and met some more of her children. Then we went to Jeanne's house. Mind you, she had only spoken to her brother (whom she had not seen in 36 years) maybe twice over those many years. Those times were since their fathers' passing. We entered the house quietly and there she was sitting, sewing. A plant display camouflaged us. She had seen a picture of me that my mother had sent, so they sent me first to the area where she was seated. She looked up and, with a priceless smile on her face, screamed, "Timmy!!!" She leapt out of her chair and gave me a hug so intense I was certain I would be left with permanent indentations on my body. Then she met everyone else and gave them the same kind of hug. I still remember that day with fond recollections just as if it had only just occurred!

The remainder of that first trip was spent touring all over the island and visiting Anguilla as well, learning where the family was and absorbing the culture and all that the islands had to offer. It was one of my greatest experiences. After that trip I have been frequenting these islands for the last 34 years. In hindsight those were rare treasured times that I keep close to me always. Toward the ends of the lives of both my Aunts Monty and Jeanne, they both said to me in separate conversations that I was their favorite out of all of their nieces and nephews, perhaps simply because I always sought them out whether in person in St. Maarten/St. Martin, or on the phone from New York. It's funny how, once I arrived and put my bags down, the first places I would head to were their houses to say I was there. It was and still is an honor to be revered in that way. Now jump ahead with me to 2000. I was walking in Grande Case, St. Martin with my parents one afternoon. I noticed this lady across the street walking toward us.

She looked very familiar because of her physical characteristics. She had a solid physique, red hair, and freckles which were a dominant trait on my grandfather's side of the family. Both of my father's grandparents had freckles, his father had freckles. My father and four of his siblings have freckles. The same four siblings have auburn to red hair. As a youngster my grandfather had red hair too. I asked my father if the woman looked familiar to him. He said, "Not really, I don't recall ever seeing her, with all the different people now living in St Maarten/St. Martin, it is almost impossible to tell who is from here anymore". But I was curious and I approached her. "Excuse me ma'am, are you originally from St Maarten/St. Martin?" The soft-spoken woman replied, "Yes I am". I said to her, "with respect to your maturity have you been in this area for a long time?" She said, "Yes". I then asked, "Who do you belong to?" She said, "I am a Vlaun, my name is Celine Vlaun". I asked, "do you know someone named Carroll Vlaun who lives in French Cul de Sac?" She said, "Yes, that is my brother." "Really?" I replied. "I was just at his house visiting him about a half hour ago. Did you know someone by the name of Mannin Arnell?" She said, "Yes, he was my cousin." I told her that he was my grandfather. Her face lit up.

She said a few kind words and she mentioned all the children's names. When she got to my father she said, "Fabbie". I interjected and pointed to my father who was standing next to me and said, "This is Fabbie right here!" She was so overwhelmed that she grabbed his head in disbelief. They hadn't seen each another since 1946. She gave him a beautiful hug then she hugged my mother and me.

Celine is a wonderful person who also provided me with a lot of information in regard to the Arnell family. She said something to me on our first meeting and ironically a few other people on that same trip made the same statement. **"We lived through the toughest of times, and we all made it through"**. These are strong words that represent a community which stuck together when life was a struggle in the 1920's and, perhaps for some, even as far up to the present. Personally, when I feel something isn't going right or I feel I am struggling, I think of those words. It gives me a different perspective on things. I too can make it through. Of course my struggles are nowhere near the level of theirs, but nonetheless they are struggles that I have to get through.

I have many stories of my experiences meeting family for the first time. Let me tell you about one which happened in 2012. I was on "Facebook", and I noticed one of my contact's friends was named Timothy like me. "Timothy Hodge" is from Anguilla and lives there. I "friend requested" him, and he accepted. He had already heard of me because he had come across my book online during his genealogical research. I introduced myself as a cousin. Tim is also a family historian, a very good one to be honest. I have learned a lot from him in the short time we have known each other. One day I telephoned him, and he seemed to be a very nice fellow. We spoke for quite a while. He wanted to be sure that we were indeed related and I respect him for that.

He ended up discovering our family connection through a clue provided in my family history book! We know for sure that his maternal great grandmother and my paternal great grandmother were sisters. But there may well be other connections, in a family as large as ours, which we still are searching for. In 2012, my wife Paula and I visited him in Anguilla and we became closer friends. We kept contact and in 2013 he and his brother Kennedy visited with us in New York. A month later we visited with him again in Anguilla.

Tim invited me to his radio talk show "Conversations" to discuss genealogy, and, live on radio, accorded me the honor of being the first paid up member of the still-not-yet-formed Anguilla Genealogical Society which he was promoting! (The Society was formally launched later that week and he was named its first president). This project has earned me another valued close friend, who, in yet another twist of fate, has kindly volunteered to help edit my book! Timothy Hodge has become a major inspiration for me to pursue my aspirations to complete this book. On a deeper note, we have become brothers. I'm proud to be associated with him so closely and proud of the impact he has had on me. Thank you so Tim.

My wife Paula Lowe Arnell is a very special woman. She must be or else I would have never married her, LOL. She has been a major support for me in all parts of my life as a spouse should be, and then some. The support she has given me in regard to the development of this project overall from as far back as when we first met has been wonderful.

Here is a funny story. Paula has a striking resemblance to my grandmother Cecile Armantine Carty Arnell who was from Anguilla. Paula's mother Mrs. Gloria Lowe has a resemblance to my great grandmother Eglantine Arnell of St. Martin. You be the Judge...

No, there is no blood relation of any kind. These are 4 ladies, from 3 different locations. My wife and my mother in law are from Guyana. The people from this area of the world share the same gene pool. This area consists of descendants of Europe, Africa, India, Asia, and Native Amerindians. The phenotypes of this area of the world are indeed blended. People of this area are just like any other region of the world. A group of people from a specific area will have a somewhat general look to them.

I learned that in 1840, Anguilla was being evacuated due to the extreme poverty. A good number of people were transported to Demerara, Guyana. I wouldn't be surprised if somewhere we perhaps may share cousins somewhere in the mix. But there is an uncanny resemblance, my wife likes to kid me (at least I hope she is) that if we are related...that we should start saving for a divorce HA HA!! Sorry babe....too late. ☺

Many of my cousins whom I have grown up with through the years are really more like siblings. Apart from the ones I have spoken of, one special one who stands out in particular is my cousin Yvonne Webster. I could write for weeks about Yvonne. Twenty – three years have passed since we first met, and in so many ways she is more of a sister than a cousin. Her home is my home when I visit Anguilla, and she is an awesome host. This will have to be my summary of her because with all of the amazing and wonderful experiences I have had with her, really...this would be a whole other book and it can only be but so big, LOL.

It is my firm opinion that when one gets to learn about their family, they learn a great deal about themselves. I come from a very diverse family. I embrace this fact whole-heartedly. My family is multinational, multiethnic, and multiracial. I like to call it the "best of all worlds". From this fact, I have taken upon myself to learn about the cultures that I come from, and even to learn about cultures which I am not a part of. I appreciate and respect people for their differences and I highly respect when they can blend their differences together and make similarities.

Every time I visit St. Maarten/St. Martin and Anguilla I meet family and establish relationships with them. I have gained so much from these experiences. I have always been made to feel welcome. These are wonderful experiences that I treasure and I enjoy speaking about them.

From the teachings of my parents, I have learned tolerance and acceptance of those different from me and at the same time, I realize they are not so different from me after all. I laugh to myself sometimes and say I can never be bigoted or prejudiced toward different types of people because there is a good chance I am being bigoted or prejudiced towards myself. I embrace and identify with all that I am composed of and make sure that my children do the same and do not dislike someone for what they are ethnically, culturally or racially. If they are going to dislike someone, their sole reason should be because of that person's poor character.

My family members on both sides have a variety of complexions. You have your "whites", you have your "blacks" and you have your "in-betweens". Honestly, I hate to categorize like this but point it out only for the sake of the discussion, so please pardon me. I am an "in-between" and I embrace and accept all as my family. One side does not go over the other. I teach my children the same. For me, our blood runs through the same veins, we are family. I have known people in families that will separate themselves because of characteristics like this. We all come from "seeds" so to speak. What makes us unique is how we grow. The fact of the matter is, we are all from the same "seeds" that connect us as a family.

I spoke before about the similarities amongst my relatives and myself, in terms of how we were raised. Cultures are made to be kept alive. I am making sure this continues with my project. Being raised with the family culture(s) in my home, they are commonplace for us and those connected to us. For example, I always learned that in Caribbean-based households, the most important rooms in the house were the dining area/and kitchen. That simple table that we eat off of has been regarded as the "hub" or the foundation of the home.

I bring this up because I recently interacted with a friend named Tanika Clarke Tempral who was getting married. As a wedding gift, my wife Paula and I got the couple a handmade tablecloth (from St. Maarten/St. Martin of all places). When I gave it to her and she opened it, I said to her that this gift represents Caribbean culture. Tanika is from Guyana and her "husband to be", Kevin Tempral, is from Jamaica.

I said, "You are continuing your lives together in a new direction. This table cloth represents all that you will go through in life together. Your dining table is where many of your life decisions will be made. Discussions of all types will be conducted there. Problems that arise will be solved there.

Triumphs will be celebrated and your family will unite, not just on an everyday or a planned basis but on impromptu ones as well. The dining table is the one place in the house that will remind you that you are a family for generations to come."

I strongly stand by those words. As our children get older and their own schedules come into play, it is normal that not every day will all be able to meet at the dinner table. But one thing my parents did, as did my grandparents and I am sure those before them did as well, was to make sure that one day out of the week, usually Sundays, there would be that one meal together. Even if one isn't hungry, one is expected to get to the table for that specified time even if it is just to have a glass of water. The fact is you are all there. I always knew this to be a strong Caribbean custom (as I believe it to be in other cultures as well) that I will always follow.

I laughed when my friend accepted the gift. She loved it and immediately said, "I have to get a piece of plastic to cover this". Instantly I thought, "yup…she is Caribbean" LOL. That was a reflection of my own childhood. We all had plastic covers on our dining tables as well as on our couches to protect them. As kids we hated them but they did preserve the fabric. Also, in just about every room in the house there is some religious symbol such as a cross or a prayer on the wall. And often, a statue of an elephant with its trunk raised facing the door.

With the concept of the dining table, I can't help but think about how my Great Grandfather Joseph Emanuel Richardson used to practice this custom every night. All of his children were to be home every night in time for dinner, especially Sunday dinner. They sat around the table dressed for the occasion. He always wore a white dinner jacket. With every meal they always had wine, a very French custom I have learned. There are moments at a holiday dinner or something formal when I seriously think of running out and buying a white dinner jacket! Ha Ha Ha. Whaaaat?? Hey...I could pull it off! ☺

The keeping of traditions are customary in any culture, for the Caribbean diaspora, it isn't any different. I spoke of the "dinner table and "kitchen" concept before. Marriage, family unity, festive gatherings, and religion are still strong customs that are carried over here, though tough to maintain. When immigrating to another country, already a lot of the customs are lost. It depends on the person or people to upkeep with their ways. They have to adapt to the new environment, keep the traditions yet blend those ways into modern society. In many ways for those who lived these experiences from wherever they came from, can cherish those memories, and only hope to be able to pass them down. Ironically, in those original countries, they too in some way are fighting to keep their traditions due to the ever changing world.

Another area of the home that I realize involved customary practices is the kitchen. When I had my cousin Simone Boyd (whom I had spoken of earlier) and her brother Danny over, I had them gather in the kitchen as we cooked. I told them, "it's great this is the first time we are meeting, but we are family, come up from the couch and join us in the kitchen since we have to finish preparing the meal, to continue getting to know one another." Well, really they were outside the kitchen because it was small, LOL. They could identify with the gathering and sampling of the food as we continued to get acquainted in the kitchen.

Some people will definitively say that the kitchen is the staple of ones' culture. There is truth to this. As I look back thru the years I think of the types of meals of the culture overall. All Caribbean cooking is basically the same but with minor modifications. At the same time each island has their own unique indigenous dishes.

Traditional meals represent the identity of the culture. Look at when people say "Italian Food", automatically people identify with the cuisine. Caribbean food is the same. Being a multi-generationally blended society overall there are a multitude of dishes. Growing up, we had different stews, coconut tarts, and seafood dishes (I didn't partake in that very much because I am not a seafood person. What a way to pay homage to my ancestors, many of whom were fishermen LOL).

For my Barbados side, signature dishes were flying fish and "cou cou". "Cou cou" consists mainly of cornmeal and Okra. It is usually served with flying fish or some other seafood. Fish cakes are another dish that we were exposed to as well. Cassava pone we mostly had that on the holidays. It's like a cassava cake. I would love to give you the recipes handed down to me. But if I were to divulge these specific family secrets, you would find my picture in the memorial section of this book….seriously. You know I have a cousin to this very day that won't let anyone in her house when preparing fishcakes? Yet we all have the same recipe. She must have a version that the rest of us do not have. They are extremely popular in the family though.

For Sint Maarten/St. Martin, and Anguilla I'll start off with Johnny Cakes. No home is without those. Callaloo soup, and various seafood dishes as well. Sugar cakes and Coconut turnovers are other traditional dishes. I grew up around all of these things. The kitchen really is a staple of one's culture. It is a major part of who you are. The dining room/kitchen concept is a practice that I have only noticed in this culture. I have known people from all over the world, close acquaintances whom I have spent a lot of time with. Perhaps they do it, but (respectfully) I have yet to witness it.

Our mourning practices are something to be spoken of as well. In Caribbean culture death is a "part of life". I grew up in a culture that death is celebrated. We mourn, cry, and are saddened. When the person passes, we still watch out for them. Meaning we light a candle in their room and leave the window cracked to allow their spirit to return to us before finally departing. It is our way of tribute. I am a firm believer in this. Ironically, our funerals are, for lack of a better term, festive. The preparation process though stressful always seem to find levity in the situation respectfully. The family and close friends step up to help and it turns into an event of good cheer and jocularity...a lot of jocularity, the kind of stuff that can't be mentioned in this book HA HA HA!

The funeral comes, the tributes and dedications are given. The "party" is still going on respectfully. The after gathering is where the bonding is really shown, great conversation, food, even a live band on some occasions. One can almost forget why they are there. When I was in my early 20's I went to a funeral. A cousin whom I was close with passed away. He lived life to the fullest. Imagine as a young man at a funeral meeting a bunch of single women. Only to find out after you established a rapport that she is your cousin, and it happens a few times on the same day. That was the downside of these kind of events. I would find myself constantly saying, "That's the end of you...Next" several times HA HA HA!. The bottom line was, we celebrate our dead and hold them in the highest honor.

I was raised to have pride in myself, to walk tall, but not to have an arrogance about myself to compromise my character. Knowledge and practice of my family's Caribbean culture plus the one assimilated from the country I was born in is not an easy task. As I said earlier, in the home was being in one culture, but once outside you had to adapt while carrying your culture with you. The United States is a "melting pot" society with so many influences.

The drawback is there is one dominant (if I may use these words) "basic culture" that all adapt to and once their kids are born here, their original cultures are compromised as the generations continue. In a matter of years, the original culture is almost erased completely for many. For my family, there are some that haven't been immune to this. Hopefully this book will build a connection for them. Having been born in the United States (I was able to maintain French rights by virtue of my father being a French citizen), I wish to keep as much of the culture alive as possible for the generations to come. Perhaps this was my grandmother's motive for asking me to keep a record of the family.

I think it is what you teach your children that keeps cultures present. The key is to hold on to what you have, and adapt it to whatever country you were born in. I have realized how you can tell a person has been brought up in or is accepting of their families culture, wherever their families derived from, simply by the way they answer a certain question. "What is your background?" If they answer, "my parents are "whatever", instantly that tells that they were not brought up in their respective cultures. It wasn't instilled, or they were brought up in that culture, but disassociate or separate themselves from it. They acknowledge their parents are that culture but they are different. My question to them is this, "Aren't you what your parents are? Were you raised by someone else?" I have yet to get an non flustered answer to these poignant questions. The worst person to allow to take away your culture, is ones' self.

I have been fortunate in that my family in St Maarten/St. Martin, Anguilla, and Barbados always acknowledged me as their family no matter where I was born. Not once was I labeled as "the American cousin", disassociating me or somehow signifying me as somehow different from them. I have always been regarded as simply "their cousin, their family". Despite being a part of the diaspora in America, I have always been regarded and respected as a St Martiner/St Maartener, an Anguillian, and a Barbadian. It is an honor to be accepted, also a cultural birthright. If there has been anyone who hasn't accepted this fact, that is their choice, but it shows their very limited knowledge and respect of my heritage and my identity. One thing that my siblings in and I have always had instilled in us was **NEVER** let anyone take away your culture, no matter who they are.

If someone had not regarded me as one entitled to carry these descriptions, I am disappointed. It is disappointing because I feel they took it upon themselves to "pigeon hole" me into being what they felt I should be to accommodate themselves. I won't allow myself to be placed in a "box" for someone else's convenience or to fit in. In short, they attempted to strip me of my culture and birth right. I have heard some say that a "would be" person is not a "real" representative of their heritage. That is the beauty of being part of a diaspora. You can still claim your culture and command respect for it. If someone chooses not to respect you for that, they are denying you of your rightful heritage. That is just to put it mildly.

If Americans of European descent can be respected as being regarded as "Italian, Irish, or German American" etc. for many generations after their ancestors arrived here, surely my "callaloo" of cultures combined being of Caribbean descent can be respected as "Caribbean American". Funnily, I was once told that I had made that term up because there was no such thing. I took it as a compliment. Imagine, I was once told I made up this name. That I created a false name for millions of people that didn't exist. I'll take that derogatory comment as a compliment because that I gave them an identity in a place that always mistakes their true identity (by calling them African American)☺.

I love my Caribbean culture for what it has taught me. I'm not saying that one culture is better than another, that would be a foolish statement. All cultures have their special qualities. But mine, for all that I have been able to experience, is a great culture to be a part of. I must say when I started this project so many years ago, I never thought that it would have gone this far. I got to learn my roots, memorize them, become an information hub for the family globally at a young age. Indeed I have spoken on the best part of the project which have been the family members I have met in person and online.

Someone had recently asked me what I have gotten the most out of doing this project. There are a number of things. Firstly, I was able to deliver a promise made to my grandmother when I was 12 years old. As kids, we make promises of all different kinds. Rarely do we actually carry them out. I like to think of her (as well as my grandfather) feeling proud and smiling down upon me. Their legacies are now in print to share with the world. They will be learned, of and never forgotten.

Secondly, I was able to reunite several generations of my family and teach them about their forefathers. Who they were, from whence they came to where we continue. Thirdly I have been able to posthumously reconnect long lost children with pictures of their parents that they had none of whatsoever. Only memories. Their offspring could now place the names with the faces of the grandparents, great grandparents, and even further back.

Finally, without trying I have had the opportunity by sheer happenstance to have been able to meet close and distant family members by accident. Simply by having a conversation, I have gained great relationships. Here is a great example. Four years ago I was working with an entertainment/publishing company. I was leaving the company to go to another position elsewhere. A young woman was hired to replace me and I helped to train her for her new position. Her name was Catania. A lovely person. We worked together briefly and in those two weeks established a friendship. Work was a priority of course but we clicked on a personal level, we spoke about lots of things from our work experiences to our children, and regular conversation. She had mentioned that her mothers' family was from Aruba and the family name she believed was Arrindell. She didn't know much about her moms' family.

I told her that my original family name was Arrindell and how it became Arnell, etc. There was a good chance that we were related. She had a resemblance to the family, and I have a lot of family in Aruba. I left the position and moved on professionally. Later that year I was on Facebook. It happened to be my birthday and I was going to wish another cousin of mine named Darlene Alias, who lives in Aruba, happy birthday because we shared the same day.

I saw a birthday wish from Catania and after wishing my cousin happy birthday, I in-boxed her and asked how did she know Catania. She said that she was our cousin. Now cousin Darlene who I had contacted happened to be the granddaughter of my grandfathers' sister. Catania and

Darlene were first cousins. We all had the same connection. Our 3 parents were first cousins. As I think back I remember showing her a little of my project. We had gotten interrupted and never had the opportunity to continue. If we had she would have seen a picture of her grandmother Marie Arnell – Alias, and we would have made our connection sooner. What are the chances that closely related cousins would meet the way that we have. This makes our story very special.

I instantly friend requested Catania and told her the great news, we had become closer ever since. We have a lot in common. She his passionate, a hard worker, has an amazing sense of humor with impeccable comedic timing (just like me ☺, which is why we clicked so well initially) and a great mom to her 17 year old daughter named Cienna. It is the stories like this that I love to share and sums up what I have gotten out of this project the most.

Lastly, one of which I must speak of is J. Hyguenec Webster. One of the most interesting and most fascinating people I have met during this project. He is from my Anguilla side of the family, he was born and lives in St. Martin. Only 23 years old and has the seasoned passion of someone way older. He has become a major component in my research of the family. He has a great talent in records research and retrieval. J. Hyguenec has taken me as far back as 6 generations before me. In the research process I have learned a lot from him. Like all of the other cousins I have met, I have established a strong relationship with him. Young Mr. Webster is a part of an elite group and I am pleased to call my friend. A special congratulations to Mr. Webster on becoming a certified registered genealogist in 2014.

Before I started my research 34´ years ago, I knew a considerable amount about my family history for someone

so young. A typical 12 year-old does not have an immediate interest in such a topic. My culture, as I stated earlier, enabled me to appreciate other cultures, and to not be bigoted or prejudiced. As I learned more about the family, I realized that many nationalities have contributed to my identity as they populated the Caribbean over the centuries.
I'm proud to say my lineage on my father's side consists of African, Irish, Scottish, Dutch, French, English and Amerindian (Arawak and Carib tribes). My mother's side consists of African, Irish, English, Spanish and Italian. I have learned a little about each of these countries and cultures through the years. I even went to the limit scientifically with my research. I took a DNA admixture test with "Ancestry by DNA". I wanted to know what were my percentages of my genetic lineage. The test concluded that my genetic makeup consisted of 51% Sub Saharan African, 44% European, and 5%East Asian. The geneticist informed me that this is where the Amerindian linage comes in. It was a very interesting experience and it was nice to see my full blend. If you can take the opportunity to do this, please do. It is worth it.

Many people have asked me through the years, how have I been able to find the time and the desire to do this. For me it was a promise I had made many years ago that I wanted to fulfill. It was never a "hobby" or a "pass time" project. It was a passion to learn as much as I could about my family that I could to preserve our culture and our knowledge of who we truly are. It has been an honor to fulfill this task. Yes, having an initial interests helps and I implore others to do so. Once a person learns a little about their past, whatever it may be, human curiosity will kick in and you will want to learn more.

I was lucky to have obtained the bulk of the information I had gotten before the popular search engines were created. I was fortunate to have been able to meet older family members who could provide me with the answers that I was searching for. For those who choose to look into their past, you will have faster results in terms of gaining information through the search engines like Ancestry.com or Rootsweb.com. If you are fortunate enough to interview the elders of your family, that is even better. You will have a firsthand account of your families' history from those who lived it, coupled with the search engines, you will be surprised to see how far you will be able to go back in researching your family. Don't get discouraged if you "run into brick walls" in your search. Keep digging, there is **ALWAYS** a paper trail. You will find it, just don't give up. I never thought I would have gotten back as far as the 1600's.

With a background like this, again I will say that it would be pointless to be negative towards any other race or culture without being negative towards myself. I love it when people ask my background, it shows that they take an interest in me, rather than make assumptions. In the world we live in, perceptions are made prematurely on so many different subjects. If people took the time to ask even a few questions and learn a little, the world would be much less judgmental.

I was once asked an interesting question, "What does it mean to you to be a Caribbean American"? I had to think about this carefully. It wasn't a question I had ever been asked before. Simply, for me it means to be part of a unique culture of people that have lived through the toughest of times and have all made it through. The knowledge, the work ethic, the will to survive in the most challenging situations. The sense of family, the "representation" of a person, to help them out, and get them on their feet. The respect instilled in us to remember that we are all God's children. To care for our elderly the way they once cared for us. All of these values have transferred from whence our parents and grandparents came. To be "traditionalized" and continued by us who are the same blood and culture as them. Subtle ways and gestures carried through the generations, not realizing that we pay homage to our forefathers by emulating them. I could have been born in Japan or the most remote location on earth. My culture would have been instilled in me the same exact way. Though it is a biased opinion, it is an honor and a privilege to have grown up in this culture. To hold on to it my entire life, and pass on to my children, and so on.

When asked, "What are you?" I like to first answer, "A child of God". Then they ask, "No, your background?" I then reply, "it depends on what I am standing in front of". After a brief laugh I simply say that I am a "Caribbean American. A very proud one!" This is what makes me a ... "Fortunate Member of a Caribbean Diaspora".

### Eternally...A Caribbean Family

Across the horizons they traveled
Whether stolen, despaired,
Or of free will.
Landing on small pieces of earth
Built communes where
They barely had their fill.
Active members of society of
All levels through determination,
Faith and fortitude.
Having the will to persevere
Ensured to survive
No matter what the mood
Roots were planted, customs born
Ways of life were now a culture
From the dawn of each morn.
Centuries passed
From crippling poverty
To a more substantial mean.
They kept moving forward
Their foresight,
Not unseen.
Came a time for some to branch out
They took their risks,
They prepared to do without.
Some went to isles nearby
Some chose the distance, float or fly
Some made it, some would die.

They carried their ways and customs,
blended their knows
with societies new.
They taught their offspring
Who, what, where they are from,
And instilled that they are this too.

As the generations pass,
Families grow in mass,
They learn their family through their fame.
But most of all,
And don't ever forget however new
How far from whence they came
And to where they will continue.

# Thank You

This page has been created to list the names of and to give thanks to all those who have contributed to this continuously growing project.

| | |
|---|---|
| Cecile Armantine Carty – Arnell | Carroll Vlaun |
| Gratien Emmanuel Arnell | Daphnie Brill |
| Mr. & Mrs. Fabien V. Arnell | Sonny Rogers |
| Mrs. Paula Arnell | Yvonne Webster |
| Iva Carrington | Cecile Sutton |
| Devern Flemming | Evan A. Lao |
| Armentine S. Laurence | Gloria Flemming |
| Jeanne E. Brill | Lionel Arnell |
| David Rodgiers | Heather Nielson |
| Eustache N. Arnell | Abraham Christian |
| Barry Rodgiers | Veronica Smith |
| Glenford Laurence | Celine Vlaun |
| Al Lake | Rose Vlaun |
| Erno Richardson | Marie Richardson |
| Ronald Lake | Yvonne Richardson |
| Carmen Carrington | Bathilda Richardson |
| Jane Douce | Jo Jo Richardson |
| Neil Kruythoff | Emile Larmonie |
| Carleton Dupont | Sandra Laurence |
| Augustain Arnell | Nilda Baly |
| Dolores Peterson | Andrena Romney |
| Emile Larmonie | Simone Boyd |
| Patricia Larmonie | Sonny Arnell |
| Gaby Richardson | Sheila Smith |
| Gloria Blount | Timothy Hodge |
| Pascal Hunt | Judith Ras-Bickell |
| Inez Shortridge | J. Hyguenec Webster |
| Fabien Gumbs | Blondell Rodgiers |
| Barry Rodgiers | Mrs. Alexander Arnell |
| Druphemia Lake | Rosa Nuzez |
| Denise Crawford | Henry Guzman |

**Philip Timothy Arnell** was born in New York, U.S.A. on October 3, 1968 of parents of Caribbean descent. He is a proud Caribbean American who holds dual citizenship with the United States and France. He resides in New York and shares his heart with the Caribbean. He has worn many hats in his lifetime. He was a child/young adult performer with an impressive resume that left him many credits in commercials, voiceovers, television, stage and motion pictures. He earned a BSc Degree in Communications in 1991 from St. John's University, New York City.

In later years, he has found his place working in the financial industry. He is a comedian, loves singing and dancing, and is a talented cook. Philip has spent the last 34 years researching, learning, and embracing his history and culture to ultimately put it in book form to share with the world. With this work he now adds another title, that of author.

Philip Timothy Arnell is a man who has been blessed with all that life has to offer - a loving family, an endearing wife, and wonderful children. These have been his motivation to record his family history and thereby fulfill a promise made to his grandmother when he was 12 years old. With this book he hopes to immortalize his ancestors both near and far, and most of all, to unite his family globally.